God's Got This!

Trusting God In The Storms Of Life

William H. Burton, III, MBA, Ph.D

WESTBOW
PRESS®
A DIVISION OF THOMAS NELSON
& ZONDERVAN

WestBow Press books may be ordered through booksellers or by contacting:

WestBow Press
A Division of Thomas Nelson & Zondervan
1663 Liberty Drive
Bloomington, IN 47403
www.westbowpress.com
844-714-3454

ISBN: 978-1-6642-8386-2 (sc)
ISBN: 978-1-6642-8387-9 (hc)
ISBN: 978-1-6642-8385-5 (e)

Library of Congress Control Number: 2022921175

Print information available on the last page.

WestBow Press rev. date: 12/12/2022

Foreword

'Cause what if Your blessings come through raindrops?
What if Your healing comes through tears?
And what if a thousand sleepless nights
Are what it takes to know You're near?
And what if trials of this life
Are Your mercies in disguise?
—Laura Story

Bill quoted this song to me several months before his passing. He committed his diagnosis and outcome to God, believing that even in the suffering, God was revealing Himself. Regardless of the outcome, he would say that God was in control and he was resting in that. Whenever I hear the phrase *"God's got this!"* I will be reminded of Bill.

I was privileged to be a pastor to Bill Burton for a number of years, and he was also on staff and part of the preaching team of Life Community Church for several years. Although I don't remember our first conversation, I can say that from my earliest recollection of Bill, he was a prince of a man. Even though I was one of his pastors, he mentored *me,* and our friendship is something that I will always cherish deeply. Most of those who knew Bill would agree that just knowing him enriched their lives, and if you listened closely when he spoke, you gained a fresh perspective of God's character and purpose for each of us.

He was also a man who knew how to live. He and Joan liked to get out and enjoy life. But more importantly than just knowing how to live physically, Bill knew how to live spiritually. He found meaning in Christ alone—and that's the part that truly defines who he was.

Shortly after Bill's diagnosis, I wanted to make sure I was spending as much time as I could with him to enjoy his friendship and to glean from his wisdom. Bill was always willing, and we took advantage of those times. It was very easy to spend time with Bill because we had shared values: Jesus and coffee (in that order). Between sips of coffee, our conversations were a mix of laughter and serious introspection and were always thought-provoking and Christ honoring. I came to think of them as "Proverbs from Bill." I always walked away with something fresh and new to ponder.

Throughout his cancer journey, and especially when he faced the nearness of death, Bill said that God began giving him grace in place of fear. As he looked into the face of death, he saw it as a defeated enemy. He would say (with a confident smile), "Satan, is that all you've got? All your weapons have already been destroyed by Jesus Christ. Death is defeated. He has already won!" When he would say that, I would think of the words of the apostle Paul in Philippians 1:21 (NIV). "For to me, to live is Christ and to die is gain."

Bill never referred to cancer as diminishing his faith in God. In fact, quite the opposite was true. It served to only *increase* his faith. "There are no pockets in running pants," he would say. "Don't focus on the things you can carry but on the race in front of you." Bill, you ran that race well, my friend.

My hope is that in the pages of this book, you'll hear the heart of a humble man of God who strove to love people and to love Jesus with all of his heart, soul, mind, and strength! These sermons and notes are born out of countless hours in research and intimate moments with God. I loved Bill as a brother, and I'm grateful for his eternal impact on my life and others who were privileged to know him. Bill is missed by so many, but his legacy lives on in his selflessness, his generosity, and his love for his Lord.

Stephen Cresse
Pastor, Life Community Church, Fort Wayne, Indiana

Preface

By Joan Burton

August 2015: I remember the day like it was yesterday. Bill and I were so excited to pick up our brand-new motor home from the dealer right here in northern Indiana. After getting some instructions, we were soon on our way! I followed Bill in our SUV as he drove this huge RV off the dealer lot and we headed back to Fort Wayne. As expected, Bill drove it like a pro! We had so many wonderful plans for this RV adventure. In just a few weeks, we planned to spend a month "on the road" celebrating our thirtieth wedding anniversary.

September 2015: We headed to Baltimore, Maryland, to visit family. We took our time getting there, spending a few days along the way to enjoy the beautiful scenery and getting more and more excited about the RV. We spent nearly a week in Baltimore and then headed south. We spent another week in Myrtle Beach, South Carolina, a favorite! Hurricane Joaquin cut our stay a little bit short. We spent several days in St. Augustine and enjoyed it very much. From there, we drove to Orlando for our family vacation at Walt Disney World's Fort Wilderness.

October 2015: Bill and I arrived at Fort Wilderness in the RV a few days ahead of our daughter, son-in-law, and granddaughter's arrival by plane. We spent a fabulous week at Disney World, and it was so fun being in the RV as a family! Toward the end of October, we drove the RV down to Fort Myers, Florida. We had previously found a lovely campground/resort there that we really liked. The plan was to leave the RV there on the campground's storage lot for a few months. We flew home at the end of October.

December 2015: After having a wonderful Christmas with the "kids," Bill and I drove our SUV to Fort Myers. We spent the next four months living in our RV at Seminole Campground and Resort in North Fort Myers. It was so much fun! We made lots of friends, found a great church, and soon developed a nice routine of working our jobs in the morning and then taking a break for some pool time in the afternoon. We were so blessed to have flexible jobs that allowed us to work from our tiny home.

April 2016: We left Florida in the RV with our SUV in tow and headed back to our home in Fort Wayne, Indiana. During the time we were in Florida, we talked a lot about how well this RV life was working for us. We both agreed the RV was more than adequate for our needs. We wanted to travel this great country! We wanted to live a simpler life, a smaller life, and find other people in other campgrounds who needed to hear about this wonderful God that we serve. We prayed about it every single day. By the time April rolled around, we knew what we were going to do! We decided to sell our very large and very lovely home, which we had built in 2000. It was way too big for just the two of us now.

June 2016: We took a family vacation in the RV to Pigeon Forge, Tennessee. We did all the touristy things and spent several days at Dollywood. While we were eating dinner one night at a BBQ restaurant, Bill said he felt like his food was getting stuck in his throat. He waited a few minutes, drank some water, and said it resolved.

July 2016: We began packing things up, fixing things, painting, etc. We gave away all of our furniture, pots/pans, dishes, linens, yard equipment, snow blower, etc. We didn't want to deal with trying to sell it so we just gave it all away.

August 2016: The house went on the market. Bill took me on a seven-night cruise to Alaska to celebrate my sixtieth birthday. It was amazing and we had so much fun. One night at dinner, Bill again complained that it felt like his food was getting stuck and it wouldn't "go down." Once again, this resolved rather quickly. Being the wonderful nurse and wife that I am, I promptly told him that he needed to slow down when he ate because he ate too fast.

September 2016: The house was *sold!* We drove the RV to Myrtle Beach for a week so that I could attend a nursing conference. One day when we were leaving the beach and walking back to the RV, Bill said he was very light-headed and felt like he was going to pass out. Since it was very hot and he was carrying the bulk of our beach stuff, we both assumed that he just got overheated. On the way back to Fort Wayne, we stopped in Ohio so that Bill could attend Indiana Wesleyan University's faculty retreat. We began focusing on getting out of the house and living full time in the RV. We planned to drive to Baltimore to visit family and then from there begin leisurely driving down the East Coast, arriving in Fort Myers by the end of October. We planned to fly back to Indiana for Thanksgiving and Christmas, but ultimately, the goal was to spend six months living in the RV in someplace warm like Florida, Texas, or Arizona, and then the other six months back in Indiana near the kids. In mid-September, Bill was scheduled for a colonoscopy. I called the GI specialist and asked if an endoscopy could be added on since he was having problems swallowing his food. The physician agreed and stated this was probably some type of esophageal stricture.

September 30, 2016: Bill just went back for his colonoscopy and endoscopy procedures. I'm in the waiting room making all sorts of lists. We close on the house in five days. I have to contact various friends about when they can come over to the house and take the pieces of furniture and other household items they expressed interest in. I have to stock the RV with food. I have to transfer our clothes to the RV. Bill is getting an eye exam tomorrow and getting the oil changed in our SUV after that. There's still so much to be done. The doctor is here and tells me that Bill's colonoscopy was great and showed no areas of concern. The endoscopy however, well that's a different story. The doctor is certain that Bill has cancer of the esophagus and tells me, "It's bad." The doctor assures me that he is going to take great care of Bill and is working on getting him scheduled for a CT scan tomorrow (Saturday). After he leaves, I'm in shock. I can't even think straight. All I can think to do is pray. I pray that this is all some type of mistake and Bill really doesn't have cancer. I started texting everyone I could think of, asking them to pray. One dear friend, who knew we had to be out of our house in five days, texted me that she and her husband would soon be leaving for Arizona for six months and she offered us their house to live in for as long as we needed to. God was providing for us even before we realized what we needed.

This book is the story of what our lives looked like over the next nearly four years. Bill endured so many tests and so much chemotherapy, radiation therapy, clinical trials, etc. He never once complained. More importantly, however, is that he never questioned, "Why me?"

After being diagnosed with cancer, Bill began a blog that allowed him to share the things God was teaching him during this storm. He looked for any and all opportunities to preach and/or share his testimony of God's faithfulness. So many friends and family members expressed just how much Bill's words meant to them. Many times, he was asked about writing a book. I think he would have enjoyed writing a book.

It has now been two years since Bill lost his battle with cancer and God chose to take him to his heavenly home. I have periodically shared on social media some of the things that Bill said or things that he wrote in his prayer journal. Once again, numerous friends and family members shared how much these comments from Bill meant to them and asked me to put these in a book. So that is what I am doing. I am not writing this book for money. In fact, every single penny from the proceeds of this book will be donated to missions, which is where Bill's heart was.

I hope you enjoy reading Bill's comments. I'm so thankful for all of his writings. It's like having him join me in my devotions and prayer time each day! He had such wisdom and keen insight. Although he's been gone nearly two years, I can still hear his words of comfort and encouragement as I try to move on in this life without him. I don't want to live in the past, but I also don't want to forget or deny that it happened. Bill's cancer battle was very difficult. That journey was a tough time. However, many blessings came out of it. Mostly, I just want to give God the glory for the great things He has done! Now more than ever, I can't wait to get to heaven.

Acknowledgment from Bill

I'd like to share a story about a missionary who came to the church Joan and I were attending in Fort Myers in the winter of 2016. The missionary ran a home for girls who have accepted Christ as their Savior. The missionary talked about those girls literally sacrificing their lives to follow Christ. Many times, they had been kicked out of their homes and ostracized from their families, with nowhere to go. They laid themselves on the altar as sacrifices to God. What stories they shared with us that evening! I began thinking about the verse in Romans about presenting ourselves as living sacrifices.

When we got back to our motor home that evening, I read through Romans 12 and let the Holy Spirit speak to me. I took some notes, read some more, prayed some more, and allowed God to teach me some very important truths about this passage of scripture. Approximately eight months later, I was diagnosed with stage 4 cancer of the esophagus with spread to the liver. I continue to receive chemotherapy even as I pen these words. When the opportunity presented itself to preach at my church for four Sundays in a row, I knew what my topic would be. You see, even though my life has been turned upside down with this cancer diagnosis, God has never let me forget about that missionary, those girls, and Romans 12. The irony of all of this isn't lost on me. In October 2016, I was given two to three months to live, yet through His infinite wisdom, God gave me a story to share about presenting ourselves as *living* sacrifices. Who says God doesn't have a sense of humor? This blog is the result of my journey through cancer and my coming to realize that in order to be living sacrifices, Jesus asks each of us to die daily.

Worst Day of My Life, So Far

As I was trying to wake up from the anesthesia, the nurse told me to get dressed and I would be wheeled back to a different part of the hospital to meet with Dr. Sharma and my wife. I knew then that I would not be getting good news. Joan should have been with me in the recovery area, but she wasn't. So it was not a huge surprise to hear the *C* word: *cancer.*

Cancer. That's for other people. I've been healthy most of my life. For years I worked hard on this body, staying in good physical shape. I keep my weight down. I've never abused by body with smoking, alcohol, drugs, etc. Maybe all that work was to prepare my body for the coming difficulties: surgery, radiation, and chemo. Joan said I'll have a ministry when this is over. I don't want that kind of ministry. But I trust my Heavenly Father in all things.

Over the years, I've learned that there are times when we get to talk about our faith and there are times we get to live it. Cancer changes one's perspective. Yesterday, I was deeply concerned about this upcoming presidential election. I'm still concerned about our country's future, but not nearly as much. Quite suddenly, my priorities have changed. Amazing. We had big plans for the next six months: close on the house, travel to Baltimore to visit family, and then spend the winter in Florida in our motor home. Why are we dealing with this now? We could have kept the house if we had known. What is God's plan now? Will we understand it sometime later? Will any of this ever make sense? We met with friends tonight for our monthly dinner club. We actually started gathering when one of the eight members was diagnosed with breast cancer and going through chemotherapy. Now maybe it's my turn to be supported by the group. It was good to be surrounded by friends—godly friends. I'm pretty sure this is how the body of Christ is supposed to function. What a thing of beauty to be a part of.

Through It All

Well, I've had CT scans of my chest and abdomen performed. I had an esophageal ultrasound. I had a PET scan performed. I also had a stent placed in my esophagus to make it easier to eat and to prevent my food from getting stuck. Yesterday, friends came by to pick up stuff they wanted from our house. Pastor Steve Cresse blessed us by taking a bunch of stuff that just needed to be thrown away. He prayed for us outside in our driveway. Thanks, Steve. What a big help my son-in-law, Seth, has been. He and his parents, Bill and Rose, have been here helping to get stuff out of the house and garage as well as clean the inside of the house. My daughter, Kerri, worked so hard packing stuff up and cleaning the house. Kerri and Seth were such a blessing. I know they went home very tired. I thank God for them and their willingness to help during our time of need.

I cut the grass for the last time yesterday at the house. This is one thing I will miss about leaving the house. No, that's not a typo. Whenever I was on my John Deere with my headphones on listening to my tunes, all was right with the world. Yesterday, Andre Crouch reminded me that "Through It All," he had learned to trust in Jesus. That's been my theme song throughout today as we closed on our house and moved into a hotel near the hospital.

Joan and I met with the oncologist, and we both instantly liked him. My cancer is stage 4 esophageal cancer with spread to the liver. He said if I do nothing at all treatment-wise, I will likely only live two to three months. However, with chemotherapy, he believes he can get me one year. One year might not seem like much, but compared to two to three months, it seemed like a gift. He also wants me to get into a clinical trial where I will either get a study drug or placebo along with the chemotherapy. I won't know whether I'm actually getting the research drug or not. Sign me up! Hopefully, I can get my port placed early next week and start chemotherapy by the end of next week. It occurs to me that I'm not in control of anything. No one asks what day or time works best for me when making appointments. I have nothing scheduled in my life that matters more than this right now. The things that matter most aren't things at all. God, people, and health matter, but things? Not so much. Dear God, please don't let me forget this valuable lesson.

A coworker sent me a text today with this verse:

> Praise be to the God and Father of our Lord Jesus Christ, the Father of compassion and the God of all comfort, who comforts us in all our troubles, so that we can comfort those in any trouble with the comfort we ourselves have received from God. For just as the sufferings of Christ flow over into our lives, so also through Christ our comfort overflows. (2 Corinthians 1:3–5 NIV)

How Are We Doing?

Many of you have asked how Joan and I are doing emotionally, mentally, and spiritually. The emotions are on overdrive. Generally, I think we are doing well emotionally, until we start talking about it. It's just so difficult to accept this as our new normal. Joan says it feels like a bad dream that we must somehow wake out of. I'm a mess of emotions when I try to talk about any of this, and I hate it.

Mentally and spiritually, I think we are right where we should be. We know that there is a good chance that my life will end much sooner than either of us had ever imagined. We also know that God, not the doctor, is in charge. We are trusting God to be who He is—our Heavenly Father. He may heal. He may not. In either case, He has promised to never leave me.

I plan to fight this cancer with all that is in me in order to prolong my life. I want to live. I want to see my grandchildren graduate from high school and college, get married, and give us great-grandchildren. I want to share the gospel of Christ with more people. I want to expand the kingdom of God. Despite what I want for my life, I submit to His will—whatever that looks like. I know that God's grace is sufficient, no matter what. I will ask Him for a lifetime and rejoice and bless Him for each day He gives me.

A Long, Dark Tunnel

Last week, Joan and I moved into Dave and Darlene's house, where we will stay for the next six months. Five days after receiving the cancer diagnosis, you may recall we closed on the sale of our house. This left us essentially homeless. We spent some time in a hotel when we needed to be near Parkview. We spent a few weeks with our daughter, Kerri, and her family in Hartford City. Our lives have pretty much consisted of bad news on top of bad news. We have been trying to process all of this and deal with it, moving around, still working, etc. Darlene and Dave were heading to Arizona for the next six months and graciously offered for us to live in their beautiful home while they are gone. What an answer to prayer. A few days before they left for Arizona, they asked us to stay with them at their home so they could go over a few things with us regarding the location of water shutoff valves, security codes, etc. Knowing we would be at their house on Sunday, they invited us to go to their church with them. I really did not want to go. I didn't want to go to a new/different church. I wanted to go to my home church, where I knew there were people who loved and supported us. But I also wanted to honor these wonderful people who were so generous in offering us their home. So we planned to go with them to their church. That morning, I wasn't feeling well at all. I came very close to playing the "sick man" card and just backing out of going to church with them. Once again, I felt checked in my spirit. I knew that going with them was the right thing to do. What follows is copied from Joan's journal regarding that weekend:

> On Saturday, the day we moved into Darlene and Dave's home, we stopped at a little park to go for a walk before arriving at their home. It was a beautiful, warm, sunny October day, and I remember thinking, *It really shouldn't be this pretty out. How dare the sun rise!* As we walked along, I began crying, explaining to Bill that I just felt as if I was in a long, dark tunnel, and despite my best efforts, I was completely unable to see the light ... any light at all. If I could just know that the ending we face with Bill's cancer would be a happy one, I really would be better able to handle all of the bad stuff inevitably coming our way. Bill looked at me and just burst out laughing! Here I am, crying almost uncontrollably, and he started laughing. He reached for my hand and said, "Joan, where's the faith in that? All of us would trust God if we always knew the outcome! It's when we don't know how things are going to turn out ... and we still choose to trust Him ... that's a walk of faith." He then stopped walking, turned to me, and said, "You want to know if everything is going to be OK at the end of this battle, right? Well, I can tell you for certain, yes, it will be. Everything will be OK. It might not be the outcome that you want, but it will still be OK. In fact, it will be better than OK. It will be great! Because it's what God wants to happen. He is in control." So we moved into Darlene and Dave's house that day and went to church with them the following day. Imagine our surprise when

the first words out of the pastor's mouth were "How many of you have ever felt as if you were in a long, dark tunnel and you were unable to see any light at the end of that tunnel?" What? I had just said the same exact thing to Bill less than twenty-four hours earlier! The sermon was amazing, and it became very clear to both of us that we were not there at that church, with those friends, listening to that sermon, all by accident. It was just the sweetest reminder from the Lord that He understood our worries and concerns and was just letting us know that He cares.

Blessings

Recently, when I saw the oncologist, I asked him how long he thought the cancer in my esophagus had been growing. He said it was probably about a year before I was diagnosed. This would have been in late summer of 2015. Two events happened at that time, which I believe God used specifically to prepare me for cancer. In the summer of 2015, I spoke for five Sundays on the "I am" statements of Jesus as recorded in the Gospel of John. One Sunday, I spoke on the resurrection of Lazarus and the "I am" statement of Jesus to Martha found in John 11:25–26 (NIV). "I am the resurrection and the life. He who believes in me will live, even though he dies; and whoever lives and believes in me will never die." Jesus had a plan for using Lazarus's death for good. God has figured out how to use tragedies in our lives for His purposes. God was preparing me to learn to trust Him on a deeper level.

Another event that happened in the summer of 2015 is this: I was in my car while listening to the radio. I heard a song called "Blessings." It was written and sung by Laura Story. The chorus goes like this:

'Cause what if your blessings come through raindrops?

What if your healing comes through tears?

What if a thousand sleepless nights are what it takes to know You're near?

What if trials of this life are Your mercies in disguise?

As I was listening to this song, God spoke to me. He asked me if I believed these words. I hesitated and responded, "I don't like it. I don't like pain, and I don't like suffering." It was as if God was sitting in the passenger seat staring at me while waiting for me to come to my senses. I knew the correct answer, but I was stubbornly hoping He would go away. He wouldn't go so finally I said, "Not my will but Yours be done." At that point, the conversation was over. Little did I know then what was happening inside my body. I know now that I was being prepared for the journey of a lifetime. I believe if we are living close enough to God, He does prepare us for difficulties.

"The Larger Our Problems Look, the Smaller Our God Will Appear"

In February 2014, I made the above statement in a message I gave on the children of Israel's first attempt at entering Canaan. Ten spies confirmed that just as God had said, the Promised Land did flow with milk and honey. However, those ten spies also said the land was filled with giants. Two other spies, Joshua and Caleb, confirmed that what the other spies said was true, but they predicted that God would be with them and the Israelites would overcome the giants (Numbers 13).

Ten spies focused on the size of the problem. Two focused on God. This difference in perspective is significant in our ability to trust God. I regularly find my thoughts drifting toward the uncertainty of my future. I sometimes struggle with questions like "What happens if I get bad news regarding the spread of this cancer?" There are so many difficult questions, and there are no good answers. When I find that I am being overwhelmed by these doubts and fears, I am reminded that I am focusing on my problems and not on God. The more attention I give to this cancer and all of the uncertainty associated with it, the larger the cancer becomes. When I shift my focus to the awesomeness of God, the doubts and fear leave. I think about the creation story in Genesis 2 and imagine God scooping up a handful of dirt while making Adam and then breathing life into him. Then I begin to worship God. The more I focus my attention on Him and His power and His love and the many ways in which He has blessed me in the past, the fears and doubts leave. My God becomes larger and larger in my sight and my problems shrink away. Where is your focus today? Are you focused on how big your problems are or how big your God is?

Lessons from Cutting Down the Annual Christmas Tree

It's hard to believe that it has been six years since I wrote this as my wife, Joan, decorated our Christmas tree. So much has happened in six years. I remember watching her as she decorated the tree and I got both sentimental and philosophical at the same time. I hope you enjoy my lessons. My daughter, Kerri, and I had a tradition of cutting down the annual Christmas tree. As I fondly thought about it, I decided that the annual trek to the Christmas tree farm had lessons that we could all learn from.

Lesson 1: Don't settle for the first good-looking tree. Kerri was always eager to get the tree selection done quickly in order to get home and start the decorating, not realizing that the secret to a great Christmas tree begins with the selection. A well-decorated Charlie Brown tree is still a Charlie Brown tree. Shortcutting the selection process gets people in trouble their whole life. Selecting the first guy who shows a girl attention is a surefire way to end in divorce court. A management textbook calls it "satisficing"—selecting the first solution that meets the minimum criteria instead of going for the best. *Take your time, and wait for the best.*

Lesson 2: A big tree in the outdoors is a gargantuan tree in one's living room. I was guilty of this more times than I'd like to admit. The tree needs to be selected in reference to the size of the room it is going in—not the room in which it currently sits. Reference is everything. Compared to Bill Gates, I'm a pauper. Compared to most of the people in the world, I'm Bill Gates. *Never lose perspective.*

Lesson 3: It is cold, windy (sometimes raining), and generally miserable cutting down a tree, but it is worth it. Christmas tree cutting is a wintertime activity, and winter in Indiana can be miserable. Rarely has it been a nice day when we cut down a tree. But when the time came for the next tree cutting, I forgot the miserable weather we endured the previous year, eager again to beat the elements in the quest for the ideal Christmas tree. Anything and everything in life worth having is a struggle to achieve. *The easy-to-obtain things in life and the mundane are easily forgotten.*

Lesson 4: *The simple things in life are usually the most memorable.* This seems contradictory to the last lesson, doesn't it? Not really. Simple and easy are different. When you think about the act of going to a Christmas tree farm and cutting down a tree, it is a pretty simple task, yet for us, it brings back the best of memories. This is different from standing in line for hours for the "must-have gift." It's not complicated or hard to plan. It is just the simple act of spending time with a child and creating a Christmas tradition that lives on in our memories.

Lesson 5: Don't forget the saw. *Failing to plan is planning to fail.* Simple does not mean it requires no forethought. A few minutes of planning saves the long trip back to get the saw.

Lesson 6: *Natural trees aren't perfect, and perfect trees aren't real.* Natural trees smell good and look good, but they do not look perfect. If you want perfection, you want artificial. That's the way it is with people. The perfect people you see on the big screen aren't real, and the real people in your life aren't perfect.

My Treatment Continues

Tomorrow, I will undergo my fifth round of chemotherapy. Two days later, on Friday, immediately after my chemo pump is disconnected, I head back to Parkview for CT scans to determine if the chemo is doing what it's supposed to do (i.e., kill the cancer). The oncologist explained that there is no point in subjecting me to chemo if it is not doing any good. For the past eight weeks, we have only had to focus on getting the chemotherapy and dealing with the side effects. Now we are facing the unknown. We are trusting God for a good report.

In many ways, I feel like I am better than I was just prior to the cancer diagnosis. I am eating more. I have more energy. I have gained back some of the twenty pounds that I had lost. I feel like the chemo is working. We are praying and believing for more than just the good news that the chemo has kept the cancer from spreading or that the cancer has shown some remission. We are believing God for a miracle—that the cancer is gone. We are grateful for all of those praying and believing with us. Nearly every single day, I learn of someone else who is praying for me. Just today, for example, I received a beautiful card signed by eleven people from a dentist's office in Baxter, Tennessee. Our good friends Maggie and Danny specifically asked their dentist and staff to keep me in their prayers.

It's just so amazing to me that people I have never even met are spending time in prayer for me. The fact that they would each write out a few encouraging words and send a card just blows my mind! Thank you all from the bottom of my heart for all the prayers, encouraging words, cards, texts, phone calls, etc. It means more to us than you will ever know. Through all of this, I want to be proven trustworthy with this—the most personal and gloriously painful journey God has ever entrusted to me.

Cancer Reminds
Me of Sin

I hate cancer. It destroys. It kills. As long as it remains alive and active in my body, it controls me. I cannot control it. In and of itself, there is nothing good about cancer. The cancer journey, however, can change us for the better. I hate cancer and want it out of my body. Sin consumes and leaves us for dead, much like an untreated cancer. The idea of allowing cancer to grow untreated seems insane to me. Untreated (unconfessed/unforgiven) sin produces similar thoughts.

How do you feel about sin? Do you see it as a cancer that destroys, or do you see it as a toy to be played with? Sin, like cancer, does not care how you view it. It destroys regardless of whether you hate it or play with it.

Cancer also reminds me of the value of living a holy, sanctified life.

We are seeing family and friends draw closer to God through this journey of mine. Please pray for other family members and friends who need to move closer to Christ.

More Lessons from Cancer

Cancer also reminds me of the depravity of this world. This world is not my home. I am not of this world. My commentary on the Gospel of John (Burge) says that when Jesus wept at Lazarus's tomb, it was because of the brokenness of creation. God never wanted it to be this way. God desired men and women to exist in right relationship with Him in peace, harmony, health, and prosperity (shalom). When Jesus saw the hurt, pain, and hopelessness of humanity, He wept. Cancer is a continual reminder to me that this is a broken world and not the place I was created to live in. He has a better place for me, and while I am in no hurry to see it, the hope of that place is inspiring.

Tomorrow, I have CT scans scheduled for 3:00 p.m. We will meet with the oncologist on December 13 for the results of the scans and to discuss further treatment options. Some of our good friends came over tonight to pray for good news on the scans and, ultimately, for my complete healing. We are grateful for all of those who are praying for us. We have never even met many of you. Thank you for your faithfulness. No one successfully battles cancer alone. "Let us run with perseverance the race marked out for us, fixing our eyes on Jesus, the pioneer and perfector of faith" (Hebrews 12:1–2 NIV).

Good News! Praise the Lord!

I got the results of my scans on Tuesday. The doctor started the conversation with a smile and said, "We have good news." What a wonderful Christmas present for us to receive! In the nearly ten weeks since the initial diagnosis, there has not been much good news from the medical community on my behalf. The chemo has reduced not only the number of active spots in the liver but has also decreased the size of many of them. Some of the spots that were present two months ago are completely *gone!* Additionally, the esophageal cancer also appears to be significantly reduced. There has been no spread to any other parts of the body.

Since the current treatment is clearly working, the plan is to continue with every other Wednesday chemotherapy treatments for another four months (six months total). We are rejoicing that progress is being made at killing the cancer. We praise God for His faithfulness to us. The doctor says that my overall health, my laboratory studies, and the fact that I am gaining/maintaining weight are all signs that we are winning this fight with cancer.

Tuesday night we did something that we have been putting off since the diagnosis. We made some travel plans. We had to plan things around my chemo, but now that we have a schedule for the next few months, we felt it was time to leave frigid northeast Indiana and head to Fort Myers in January. Fort Myers is where we had planned to spend the entire winter. We look forward to revisiting the area, being warm, and meeting up with Joan's cousin Donna and her husband, Tom. We regularly praise God for the many kind folks who are lifting us up in prayer. Thank you for your faithfulness. Your prayers are making a difference. Please continue to pray for me as I continue to battle cancer with the Lord's help.

Valley Experiences

I spent some time last week with my IWU colleagues. What an uplifting time it was to be with so many people who have been praying for me during this journey. I appreciated the times when my colleagues asked if they could lay hands on me and pray right there in our meetings. As part of our time together with the DeVoe School of Business faculty, we had a team-building exercise in which we were asked to "share a time when you experienced God in a very special way." In my group of about ten faculty, without fail and without prompting, they shared stories (many with a great deal of emotion) of times when they went through very difficult times. In each case, it was in the lowest part of a valley experience that God was most special to them. Isn't that the way it is? When we are on the mountain, we don't rely on God as much as we do in the valley. Oftentimes when we are on the mountaintop, we accumulate junk in our lives that can distract us. In the valley, we generally strip down to the bare essentials, allowing ourselves more time for sweet communion with God that we so badly need. The hurriedness of life on the mountaintop prevents us from having that time of sweet communion with the God of peace. For each of us, the mountaintop experience should be a time of preparation or training for the next valley experience. Joan and I are still working our jobs, making time for family, medical appointments, and the other activities that we did prior to my cancer diagnosis. The difference is priorities. Quiet time, alone with God, has become a top priority. In the past, I used to fit quiet time around the rest of my life. Now it begins the day. How is your quiet time with God? I'm not talking about the shopping list of all the things we want God to do for us. I'm talking about being quiet in His presence, praising Him for who He is, worshipping Him, and loving Him. Make time today to be alone with Him. It will likely prove to be the best thing you do all day.

Merry Christmas

I forgot to write about a praise from last week. While I was getting out of my vehicle on Saturday at Indiana Wesleyan University's graduation ceremonies, I slipped on the ice. I was opening the door when both feet slipped out from under me. I landed hard on my lower back and bottom. Of course, I felt immediate pain where I fell, but nothing was broken. I had no trouble getting up, which was good since no one was around to assist me. For about an hour, I felt some discomfort, and then it slowly passed. After that initial discomfort, I was never in pain. None at all. Praise God! What is so special about this is the fact that a broken bone could have significantly set back my chemotherapy treatments. Keeping the rest of the body healthy during chemo is very important. Colds, the flu, and certainly broken bones need to be avoided in order to stay on schedule with chemo. I praise God that I had no pain, no bruises, and no negative impact from this fall. God has been so good throughout this journey.

We will be celebrating Christmas with my daughter, Kerri, and her family tomorrow. I'm sure it will be a wonderful day of celebrating the birth of our Savior. This Christmas will be extra special for Joan and me because without the healing touch of the Lord, quite frankly, I wouldn't even be here. Thank you again for all the love, prayers, cards, texts, emails, and phone calls. I am humbled and blessed by all of them. Merry Christmas to you all.

Negative Thoughts

We had a great trip to Baltimore visiting family over the Christmas holidays. We ate too much, stayed up too late, slept in, and in general, enjoyed ourselves immensely. There were times when it almost seemed like previous Christmas trips to Baltimore—before my cancer diagnosis. Everyone out there has been praying so faithfully for Joan and me. It felt so good to hug them and offer my sincere thanks.

Today was my seventh round of chemotherapy. Everything went well and I was done in just six hours. Everyone at Parkview has been so caring and professional. I am very happy with everything and feel very blessed to be getting my treatments there.

Despite the upbeat tone of my blog and other messages I send out, there are times when I deal with negative thoughts and doubts. I've learned to manage these and want to share what is working for me. It is essential (foundational) that I spend time in God's Word and in prayer. It is also important to me to meditate on God's greatness. Focusing on just how mighty, powerful, loving, and concerned God is keeps all my problems in their proper perspective. He is mighty and powerful, and my cancer is small and weak in comparison.

There are still those times, however, when negative thoughts creep into my mind, despite my belief that God will heal me. I refuse to dwell on the negative thoughts. As my pastor back in Ellicott City,

Maryland, used to say, "You can't stop the birds from flying over your head, but you can keep them from building a nest in your hair." We absolutely can control what we think about! Sometimes I choose to just get busy with other things and the negative thoughts pass. Other times, however, they linger. If I continue to struggle with negative thoughts, I start worshipping God. I go back to my foundational beliefs. I refuse to dwell on the unknowns in my current situation. I remind myself of how faithful God has been thus far. When I remember His faithfulness in the past, I know my future is secure in Him, even though I can't figure it out. To be honest, this is hard because I like to figure things out. I choose to rest in the confidence that He will be just as faithful in providing for us in the future as He has been in the past.

What about you? How do you handle negative thoughts?

Trip to Fort Myers

We were in Fort Myers, Florida, last week. We flew down and rented a condo on the beach. We really enjoyed the sunshine and warm temperatures as we sat on the beach each day. We felt so blessed to be able to get away from our routine in Fort Wayne.

The trip started out a bit melancholy when we arrived in Fort Myers on Sunday. As we drove from the airport to one of our favorite restaurants, we began to reminisce about our four-month visit to the area last year. That soon turned to sadness as we began to feel cheated by what cancer has taken away from us. We were supposed to be here for six months, not just one week. We were supposed to be living here, not just visiting. It was easy to feel robbed and cheated of what we were supposed to have.

Later that evening, as we talked about our trip, our attitudes changed as we began to focus on how we had seen God's hand at work on this trip. As followers of Christ, we don't believe in coincidences. Instead, we choose to believe that God has once again demonstrated that He is with us. Let's see how many ways we were blessed on that trip.

1. I paid for our gas on the way to the Indianapolis airport with a gift card one of our friends gave us (unexpectedly) for giving them some of our furniture.

2. When we checked into the hotel at the Indianapolis airport, we were upgraded to a nicer, larger room at no additional charge.
3. Our parking at the airport was free because we had earned enough credits from prior flights.
4. We flew Southwest Airlines and forgot to check in exactly twenty-four hours ahead of time. We were concerned that we might not be able to get two seats together on our full flight. There were 117 people ahead of us on the plane, but one of the exit rows had two seats together. I had the very seat on the plane that I would have selected if I could have picked any seat.
5. When we checked into our condo for the week, we were once again upgraded to a more spacious room on a higher level with a better view than the one we paid for.

We can focus on what we don't have or choose to focus on how we have been blessed. Our circumstances did not change between the time we felt robbed and the time we felt blessed. Only our attitudes changed. Lord, help me keep my focus on You, the author and perfector of my faith.

The Family of God

While Joan and I were in Fort Myers recently, we were able to meet up with some friends we met last year in Florida at the campground Bible Study. They were gracious enough to come to Florida a few days earlier than they had planned so that we could spend some time together. What a blessing they were to us as they encouraged us and prayed with us. Thank you, Allan and Jo Ann, for your support.

I couldn't help but be reminded after we left visiting Allan and Jo Ann that God has called us to live in community—not in isolation. We met this godly couple because we chose to join a Bible study. If we had not joined the study, we would likely never have met them. They would not have been able to use their gifts to bless us, and we would have missed out on a blessing. To be honest, I don't remember anything that I learned in that study of Galatians. I do remember, however, the impact that several of the people in that study had on us.

This is one of the reasons our church attendance is so important. God's gifts were given to build up the body of Christ. We can't use our gifts if we are not connected to the body. It is difficult for the body to minister to us when we are disconnected from the body. When I stay away from church, it means I can't use my gifts and others miss the opportunity to use their gifts to minister to me.

Ministry is also lacking if I rush into church just before it starts and leave as soon as the pastor dismisses the congregation. We are called to be connected to each other in Christ. I am so very thankful for my church family.

Good News

Today, I received round 8 of chemo. We received some really good news from the oncology nurse. Each time I receive chemo, blood is taken for lab work to determine if my body is capable of receiving chemo and if any adjustments need to be made to my treatment plan.

The nurse said that the labs today were "beautiful." The liver is functioning well in spite of the cancer and the chemo. She also stated that it is "very unusual" for a patient receiving my chemo regimen to have gone this far (nearly four months) without having the chemo dialed back due to side effects. My response to her was "I'm praying a lot." She then said, "Well, it's working! Keep doing what you are doing."

There is nothing else to account for my success thus far except for prayer. If I am having "unusual" success, then it is because God is working on my behalf. I'm not involved in any other treatments, supplements, or diets—just chemotherapy and God. So if the chemo is working better than it usually does, it must be God.

> I will exalt you, my God the King; I will praise your name forever and ever. Every day I will praise you and extol your name forever and ever. Great is the Lord and most worthy of praise; his greatness no one can fathom. (Psalm 145:1–3 NIV)

More Good News

I had round 9 of chemo today. I also saw the oncologist as I do about once a month. He was beaming with good news. My labs continue to improve, and most were completely normal today! This means that my liver function is improving. The physical exam results and my answers to the doctor's questions today all confirmed that the treatments and God are healing me. The side effects are not severe enough to reduce the chemotherapy, so the treatment plan remains the same—no reduced chemo. Praise be to God. Our prayers are making a difference. The next scans are on February 6, 2017, and we get the results two days later. We are believing that the scans will confirm that God and I are winning this battle over cancer. Thank you, as always, for your love and prayers.

The Power of Prayer

Prayer time is essential for me. You can search the gospels and see how often Jesus went away to pray. Think about that for a minute. If Jesus, the Son of God, felt that prayer time was necessary, how necessary is it for us? Years ago, I learned a prayer model that has served me well. You can Google it and learn more about it. It is called the ACTS prayer.

<u>A</u> – Adoration: Adoration looks a lot like our worship time here on Sunday morning. It's a time to praise and exalt God. It's a time to tell God how much we love Him. It's a time to express just how much we appreciate Him. Adoration helps me keep God and my problems in perspective. I need a really big God to heal me, and the bigger God is to me in my prayer time, the greater my faith and the greater the peace that I have.

<u>C</u> – Confession: Confession for me is a time of reflection and contrition. Obviously, any unconfessed sin needs to be addressed here. However, it is also a time to address any areas of my life that are not pleasing to God. I allow the Holy Spirit to speak to me about things that I might need to work on.

T - Thanksgiving: Thanksgiving has become a time of remembrance for me. In the five months since my diagnosis, we have seen God's hand at work in so many areas of our lives. Remembering God's faithfulness keeps us grateful and gives us hope. We need to be grateful to God for all that He has done. God deserves our gratitude. Spend time each day just thanking Him for past answers to prayer. This is a great way to remind yourself of His faithfulness. The God who delivered me in the past is the same God who can and will deliver me in the future.

S - Supplication: For me, supplication is praying for my healing and then mostly praying for the needs of other people who need encouragement, healing, or salvation. When I consider the value of this model of prayer, I think its most important feature is that it gets our supplication in the right perspective. It is only after I have placed God high on His throne and reduced myself to the mere speck of dust that I am ready to begin asking for things.

Great News! Praise the Lord! Thank You, Jesus!

In October 2016, there were two large tumors/lesions in my liver and multiple, diffuse, scattered, smaller lesions in the liver. Now there is only one tumor, and it has shrunk by a third! The other large tumor/lesion is gone! All of the other scattered cancerous lesions are gone! "Resolved" is how the doctor worded it. The esophagus is also showing signs of healing with the tumor shrinking considerably. The esophageal cancer has never been especially concerning to the doctors. They were always more focused on the liver. The esophageal tumor has shrunk so much that the stent that was placed several months ago has now shifted downward because it is no longer butting up against the tumor.

Praise God! The doctor and his nurse were practically giddy today with sharing this wonderful news. The doctor said it is very unusual to see this kind of improvement after only four months of chemo. He went even further and called my improvement a "statistical outlier," meaning that the results are beyond what the chemo treatments alone are capable of doing. God is at work here.

A CEA blood level (the tumor marker) should be zero or close to it. Last October, mine was nearly 1700! In December, it was 550.

Today, it is 65, which is a 96 percent reduction. Praise God! The oncologist said that every angle (i.e., the CT scans, the CEA blood levels, my normal physical exam, the minimal side effects, my ability to receive the full dose of chemotherapy for this entire time, etc.) indicates that I am winning!

The plan is to continue with chemotherapy for three more doses over the next six weeks, which will be a total of six months. Then the maintenance chemotherapy begins. Maintenance chemo looks pretty much the same as my current chemo treatment, minus one really nasty drug. So I will still have to go to chemo every other Wednesday. I will still come home with the chemo pump and have the bag of chemo infusing at home for two days. This maintenance chemotherapy will likely continue indefinitely.

So we are overjoyed with this good news! Thank you all so much for your prayers! Victory is ours! God is so good! We give Him all the glory, honor, and praise. Chemotherapy can only do so much. The rest is God!

Praying Specific Prayers

A few years ago, a visiting pastor spoke at my church on the topic of prayer. He encouraged everyone to think of a heavy object being held by a rope. He said our prayers should be like rifle shots at that rope, shooting it from many different angles or perspectives. With this thought in mind, my prayers have changed over the past few months from general prayers for my healing to very specific prayers. I pray that God allows me to tolerate the chemotherapy with minimal to no side effects. I pray that He protects my good cells from the side effects of chemotherapy. I ask God to destroy every cancerous cell in my body. I ask that He take away the cancer's source of nutrition. I pray that He supercharges the chemotherapy to make it do above and beyond what it is capable of doing. Sometimes I get carried away and ask God to hold open the cancer cells' little mouths and drown them in chemo!

Now I know that cause and effect is almost impossible to prove, so I want to tread lightly here. As I stated previously, we got some really good news this past week about the reduction of cancer in my body since the initial scans were taken last October and the follow-up scans in December. According to Joan's journal notes, after the scans in December is when my prayers got more specific. Think about that. I encourage you to pray very specific and detailed prayers.

Nobody

A few weeks ago, I had the last full treatment of chemo. From now on, I will be on a maintenance dose. For the past six months, I was able to receive twelve rounds of the full-dose chemo without needing to have the dose reduced due to side effects. We had no idea how significant being able to withstand those twelve rounds of full-dose chemo was until my last visit. We had previously been told that it was "unusual" for someone to make it to eight rounds of chemo without needing to have the dose adjusted or reduced. At my last visit, I asked just how unusual it was. The answer I was given was "Nobody in our study has ever made it to twelve rounds without a reduction. You are the first." Nobody! Praise God. How amazing is that? God is so good. We do not know what the future holds. It has always been in God's hands. We trust Him completely.

Friends

We have been doing lots of traveling in our motor home. We are currently in Branson, Missouri. Several weeks ago, we went to Baltimore to visit with family. Afterward, we drove to Tennessee to visit our friends Maggie and Danny. I am so grateful to God for good friends. Our good friends Darlene and Dave let us live in their beautiful home for six months. We moved out just a few weeks ago and into our motor home for the summer. The nights before I have chemotherapy and for the following two days, it is important for us to be near Parkview's Cancer Center. Our good friends Jim and Shelley have been gracious enough to allow us to park the motor home on their property. They live just a few minutes from Parkview, making chemotherapy and the disconnect two days later so much easier. There are so many other friends who continue to be a blessing to us. As always, we remain so thankful for all your prayers and words of encouragement. I simply can't tell you how much it means to me. There are no words to adequately describe my gratitude. God is so faithful! Amen?

Jehovah Rapha: The God Who Heals

On June 9, I had the esophageal stent removed. This was placed back in October in order to help my food advance past the cancerous esophageal tumor. Over time, as the tumor began to shrink, the stent began migrating into the stomach. The doctor who removed it last Friday looked all around the esophagus and stomach and took a sample of the former tumor area for a biopsy. The doctor told Joan that everything he saw looked to be free of cancer. Today, we got the results of the biopsy, which indicates no cancer in the esophagus or stomach! Praise God! He is so good. Please continue to pray for complete healing of my liver. We serve a great, big, awesome God. He is more than able to deliver me from this disease. Thank you for your continued support.

Psalm 91

I spoke last Sunday at church on Psalm 91. This psalm has been such a comfort to Joan and me during our journey through cancer. The below points summarize what I believe Psalm 91 is telling us:

1. God is with us in times of trouble and will deliver us.
2. The wicked will be afflicted and punished but the righteous will not have to go through that.
3. God's presence is a place of safety and security to those who remain in Him.
4. We need not be afraid of troubles because God has promised to protect us.

I guess there are two reactions to this psalm. Some, like Joan and I, actually take great comfort in it. However, some people may feel there is a disconnect between what they have experienced and what the psalm says. Some may feel that God has not provided shelter from life's troubles. Some may feel that God has allowed terrible things to happen to them just like things happen to unbelievers.

Since God and I are battling stage 4 cancer, I feel I am uniquely qualified to address those who think there is something wrong with this psalm.

Nowhere in this psalm does it say that we will not experience trouble. Nowhere does it say that the children of God are not going to suffer. It does promise, however, that God is there for us during these difficult times. Joan and I have experienced this time and time again over the past nine months. God has walked with us. He has provided for us, sometimes even before we knew we needed something. We have experienced His shelter, His refuge, and His rest. We understand what it is like to be fearful. Sometimes I can get all worked up over my situation.

There have been many times when we have been unhappy with something the doctor said. For example, he said I would have to have chemotherapy every other week for the rest of my life. We were very disappointed when we heard that. Where did we find refuge from the discouragement and fear? In God and His Word. The more we focused on Him and His faithfulness to that point in our journey, the less fear and discouragement we felt. In a very short time, Yahweh again became the center of our attention—not cancer, chemo, life expectancy, or any other disappointment. The more we focus on God and His name, the bigger He becomes in our sight and the smaller our problems become.

Undercover Boss

One TV show that I enjoy watching is *Undercover Boss*. Each episode follows the CEO of a company while he or she takes a week out of the corporate office to work the lowest level jobs within the company in disguise. The supervisors and coworkers are told that a TV crew is following a worker who has lost his or her job and is starting over at the bottom of the company in an entry level job. In each episode, the CEO finds that there are some really hardworking people doing these difficult, low-paying jobs. Each CEO has been impressed with most of the people employed by the company. In some cases, the CEO has encountered management people who have not properly portrayed the type of management philosophy the CEO wants displayed.

At the end of every episode, the CEO has the employees come to the corporate office where the CEO's true identity is revealed. To the good, hardworking employees, the CEO gives them something to show his gratitude for their hard work. The supervisors who have not been good representatives of the company have been chastised by the CEO, and in at least one case, a supervisor was told to change or leave the company.

As a student of management, I like watching the show. Most of the CEOs are terrible at manual labor. I appreciate CEOs who are willing to leave the corporate office to see what really goes on their companies. Southwest Airlines's former CEO Herb Kelleher did not need a TV show to encourage him to get out and mingle with the employees. He was renowned for showing up at an airport to throw bags with the baggage handlers or work at the ticket counter. While there, he not only understood the work the employees were doing but also engaged them in conversation. Sam Walton routinely drove his pickup truck to Walmart stores to see firsthand what was going on. Harley-Davidson requires its executives to go to motorcycle rallies to spend the weekend with HD customers, talking to them about their bikes.

The only way to know what is going on is to get out of the office and go see how the work gets done. The Japanese term is *gemba,* which means "the real place." Japanese managers are known for spending a great deal of time on the production floor. They want to see what is going on in their businesses.

Jesus came down from His "office" to see what living in this world was really like. He took the lowest level job in the universe—that of servant. He then took the job that no one else could do. He became the sacrifice for sin—not His sins but our sins. We should have to die for our sins, but He became the sinless sacrifice for our sins.

Take some time today to carefully consider the sacrifice that Christ made to set you free of sin and to make you a candidate for heaven.

It's Not Fair!

A few years ago, a friend sent me one of those emails that we all get describing one of those really unfair, unpublicized human interest stories. The email described the life of Irena Sandler, a German who smuggled children out of Poland during World War II. She is credited with saving thousands of children from death. She was imprisoned and tortured by the Nazis for her humanitarian efforts. She was considered for a Nobel Peace Prize in 2007, but the award went to someone who was far less deserving (in my opinion). How unfair!

But who said life is fair? I know my mom didn't when I was a little boy and complained of being treated unfairly. I bet your mom didn't promise you that life would be fair. How did we develop the expectation that life should be fair? Some are born smart, some are born attractive, some throw a football, and some seemingly have little in the way of talent or ability. Life is not fair.

Throughout the Bible, we see that God evaluates people by a different standard. Luke 21:1–4 tells of the widow who gave all that she had in the offering. Jesus recognized this and pointed her out as putting in more than all of the others who gave that day. Matthew 6:1–4 tells us to make certain that we do our good deeds in secret—not seeking attention. Those who do so will receive their reward from God.

Paul writes in Colossians 3:23–25 (NIV),

> Whatever you do, work at it with all your heart, as working for the Lord, not for men, since you know that you will receive an inheritance from the Lord as a reward. It is the Lord Christ you are serving. Anyone who does wrong will be repaid for his wrong, and there is no favoritism.

Don't be discouraged because you are working hard but are unnoticed. Seek God's approval of your life. Look for eternal rewards.

What a Difference
a Year Makes

This week is the one-year anniversary of receiving my cancer diagnosis. As much as we want to focus on the present and the future, we can't help but think back to those very dark days just one year ago. God has been so good to us this past year. He is so faithful, and we are so very blessed. The Bible tells us that He promises to never leave or forsake us. When you read that or when you hear that, do you really believe it? It's true. You can believe it! He never lies. He never leaves us. He never has and He never will.

Joan and I have felt His presence with us each and every day of this cancer journey. We have never known one minute of time when we didn't feel His presence. He gives us strength, courage, patience, peace, grace, and love every day so that we can go through this journey. While we appreciate medical research and skilled doctors, our hope does *not* rest in them or the health care system. It is not in chemotherapy or clinical trials. Our hope rests in God and God alone. While everything looks good on my scans at this time, the oncologist says that there is no cure for this cancer. God is my source of a cure. Thank you for your prayers and words of encouragement. We have felt every single one of them.

Scarcity Mentality

Your hardworking neighbor comes home with a brand-new luxury SUV. One of your in-laws gets a big promotion with a big, fat raise. What's your reaction to the success of others? Are you happy for your neighbor? Are you happy for your in-laws? Or are you just a little bit jealous? Do you find yourself resenting other people's success? You might be suffering from scarcity mentality.

Imagine as a child you and a sibling are staring at the last piece of pie. There are only four ways for this scenario to play out. You could get the last piece. (You win.) Your sibling could get the last piece. (You lose.) Neither of you could get the last piece. (Dad wins; kids lose.) You could share the last piece. (Compromise.) This fighting over the last piece of pie is representative of the scarcity mentality. According to Stephen Covey, this is a zero-sum game. In this worldview, everything in life is limited. In this system, the more one person gets, the less someone else gets. It is the belief that socialism and communism are founded on. This belief affects our ability to be happy for others, even people we love.

There is another way to view the world, especially in a free, capitalistic society, which of course is fading fast in the US. Stephen Covey calls this the abundance mentality. This is a belief that there is plenty for everyone. Consider the pie scenario from before. If there were another pie in the refrigerator, then there would be no dispute. We all win and we are all happy.

How does this scarcity mentality play out? If I am jealous of my neighbor's success, it might be because I think that I deserve that success. That's scarcity mentality. Did my neighbor's success prevent me from being successful? Of course not. If my in-law gets a big promotion, why shouldn't I be happy? That promotion did not come at my expense. If my neighbor wins, I don't lose. Instead it should be a sign that the system still works. Those who work hard are being rewarded.

In an extreme case of scarcity mentality, I will view everyone's success as hurtful to me. I can't be happy when someone I love has lost weight and I haven't. I fail to compliment someone on a new hairstyle or a new look because I am so unhappy with the way I look.

What does God have to say about this? Paul told us,

> Rejoice with those who rejoice; mourn with those who mourn. Live in harmony with one another. Do not be proud but be willing to associate with people of low position. Do not be conceited. (Romans 12:15–16 NIV)

If I can't rejoice in the success of others, if I can't be happy for others, that speaks volumes about me. Pride, jealousy, or maybe just a wrong relationship with the Father is preventing me from the joy that could be mine. Is God limited? Certainly not! God also says,

> Bring the whole tithe into the storehouse, that there may be food in my house. Test me in this, says the Lord Almighty, and see if I will not throw open the floodgates of heaven and pour out so much blessing that you will not have room enough for it. I will prevent pests from devouring your crops, and the

vines in your fields will not cast their fruit, says the
LORD Almighty. (Malachi 3:10–11 NIV)

Father, today help me to focus on my blessings and not my wants. I am most happy when serving You and not when I am acquiring material goods. Bless my neighbors, and bless my family and friends as you see fit. My hope and my trust are in You.

Bill's Christmas Message 2015 (Nine Months before the Cancer Diagnosis)

I feel humbled and filled with sincere gratitude to have the opportunity to share God's Word with you good folks at Life Community Church today. I want to thank Pastor Duane for his willingness to share his pulpit, and I thank each of you for remaining in your seat, even after you learned that I would be speaking. I'm so very glad that I'm a part of the family of God. It's such a beautiful thing.

It had been over four hundred years since God had spoken to His chosen people, Israel, in any significant manner. Many religious people had become indifferent toward God. Where was He? Why was He so quiet? Why did He allow these Syrians, Greeks, and Romans to occupy their land? Where was God? Had He abandoned His people? Had God perhaps had enough of their infidelity? Had God Almighty run out of patience with the very people He had chosen?

In many ways, the thoughts of the Judean people in the first century are not much different from the thoughts of people today.

Where is God? Where is He when terrorists strike? Where is He when a child is terminally ill? Where is God when I am so desperately in need of Him?

The birth of Jesus, as recorded by Matthew, includes this passage from the first chapter, verses 22–23 (NIV):

> All this took place to fulfill what the Lord had said through the prophet: The virgin will conceive and give birth to a son, and they will call him Immanuel—which means God with us.

Matthew repeated a prophecy written by Isaiah over seven hundred years prior to the birth of Jesus. "The virgin will be with child and will give birth to a son and will call him Immanuel" (Isaiah 7:14 NIV). I don't know how many times I have read this, especially during the Christmas season, and never given it much thought. How about you? Have you ever given this idea of "Immanuel" much thought?

Immanuel or Emmanuel is more than just the name of a church down the street. It means "God with us." God *with* us. It's not God against us. He is with us. He is here. God's plan from creation has always been to be with us. God loves humanity. God loves us. I don't understand why, but I do understand that He loves us. All of us, all of the time.

But sin came between man and God and separated us from God. God had a plan to reveal Himself to humankind through Israel, His chosen people. As we know, they failed. The Israelites were too inconsistent in their relationship with God to reveal much about Him, so God came and brought a new plan, a new relationship, and a New Covenant. The birth of the Christ child that we are celebrating is all about God's attempt at restoring creation to its rightful order. God and His creation in right relationship again.

Immanuel, God with us. God did not send Jesus to us to be His ambassador. God instead sent Himself to be with us. Jesus told us repeatedly (John 10:30, for example) that He and the Father are one. One God. One plan. God with us.

God came down as our Christmas present to bridge the gap between Him and us. Through His sacrificial death on Calvary, the gap has been bridged. There's just one problem: we must accept that gift. The price has been paid. The gift has been purchased. It sits under the tree awaiting us, but we must accept it. It will not be forced upon us.

On Christmas morning, would you really leave the best present under the tree wrapped and unopened? Of course not! At the very least, it would be rude to the person who provided the gift. Where is God? He is here. He is with us. He is for us. He desires that we be on the same side. He desires time with us. He desires us. Open His gift today.

Merry Christmas.

Applause

My wife, Joan, and I have always enjoyed taking cruises. We typically cruised to the Caribbean during the winter. Most evenings on the ship, we attended the evening entertainment. Several times, one of the entertainers or the cruise director encouraged the audience to give our generous applause to the entertainers if we enjoyed what they were doing. Several entertainers said something like "The more you applaud, the harder we work."

My first thought was *The entertainers are getting paid to do their best. Why should I have to applaud to get them to work harder?* Then I thought some more about it. What a lesson in life! Don't we all appreciate some applause once in a while? Wouldn't we all work (or try) a bit harder if people were applauding our efforts?

The leadership and motivation literature is totally supportive of the value of encouragement. Transformational leadership researchers Kouzes and Posner in their book *Encouraging the Heart* wrote that when asked the question "When you get encouragement, does it help you perform at a higher level?" 98 percent of respondents said yes.

Sports fans understand the concept of encouragement. Fans generally believe that they can influence the outcome of a game. That's why they yell and scream the way they do. The oddsmakers for NFL betting regularly give 3.5 points to the home team because of the impact of the home field advantage. Much of the advantage is due to the home crowd cheering for their team.

The Bible speaks of encouragement. Proverbs 25:11 (NIV) says, "A word aptly spoken is like apples of gold in settings of silver." There are no more fitting words than those of encouragement. Look for someone to applaud. Catch someone doing something well and reward them with a thoughtful word of appreciation. Encourage someone today.

Lessons I've Learned as I Go through Cancer Treatment

Lesson 1: Trust in God

In the good times, we talk about our faith, but in the difficult times, we get to walk in faith. My trust in God is, without a doubt, what has sustained me. Because my trust is in God and not doctors, chemotherapy, alternative treatments, or anything other than God, I only need to go where I am led. It is my belief that my job is to do all that I can to remain healthy and then leave the rest to God.

Lesson 2: Peace

In the storms of life, we want the rain to stop. We want the wind and the lightning to cease. We want the pain to stop. We want everything to return to the way it was before the storm. We cry out to God to fix it and fix it now! Sometimes God intervenes and the pain stops. However, sometimes He does not stop the storm. Sometimes God says, "I love you too much to allow you to avoid this lesson or this time of communion that we are going to share together." I have learned that peace does not ignore the fact that it is raining, the wind is still blowing, and the lightning is striking all around us. Peace is knowing that despite the reality of the storm, there is a greater reality and confidence in the One who can calm the storm. Peace is the tranquility to stand in the storm and know, without question, that everything will be all right. Peace is not found in the calm. Peace is knowing that Jesus is in the storm with me. Only then can I be content knowing that He is control. Real peace is attainable only in Christ. There is no security outside of Him. None. Period.

Lesson 3: Control
We want to be in control of our lives. We want to know what we are going to be doing tomorrow, the next day, and the week after that. We love our calendars that we think are controlling our lives, but control is just an illusion. We actually have very little control of our lives. In one short conversation with the oncologist, nearly every aspect of my life was out of my control. I quickly realized that one of the major problems I had with the whole cancer diagnosis was my loss of control. I could no longer make concrete plans. I hated not being able to think beyond a two-week chemotherapy schedule. The more I thought about it though, the more I realized that I was never in control to begin with. I thought I was, but the fragile nature of this life and the lives of those we love really makes control impossible. The quicker we accept that only God is in control, the easier it will be to work through life's difficult times. We may not be in control, but we are loved by the One who is. He is in control of everything and we are in control of nothing. He is God, and I am not.

Lesson 4: Storms and Quiet Times
In our storm experience, Joan and I have found that quiet time alone with God has become an essential part of our day. We still have many of the same demands on our time, as we had prior to the cancer diagnosis. We both continue to work full-time jobs. The difference is priorities. In the past, I used to fit quiet time with God around the rest of my life. Now it begins the day. When I talk

about quiet time, I'm not talking about the shopping list of all the things we want God to do for us. I'm talking about being still in His presence, praising Him for who He is, worshiping Him, and loving Him.

Lesson 5: Preparation

Several times in Paul's writings, he compared the life of service to God as a race. A serious runner would never just show up on race day without preparing. Every serious runner has a training program. Have you looked at clothing for runners? It's extremely lightweight. The serious race is meant to be run stripped down of all the unnecessary weight. In the difficult times of life, we get stripped down to the bare essentials. The difficult times in life are not the times to try to figure out our relationship with God. That is not the time to develop our personal theology. It is not the time to try to understand why bad things happen to Christians. The mountaintop experiences, when things are calm, should be times of preparation for the next difficult time in our lives. My experience with cancer has been so much easier to handle because of the time I spent in preparation *before* I received the diagnosis and not even knowing what the difficulty would be. My relationship with God was good prior to the diagnosis. My body was in good shape to handle the treatments. When we are on the mountaintop, we tend to rely on ourselves and not on God as much as we do in the valley. Oftentimes when we are on the mountaintop, we accumulate junk in our lives—junk that ultimately distracts us. It is in the valley, my friend, where we strip down to the bare essentials, allowing ourselves more time for sweet communion with God that we so badly need.

Don't Limit God!

As you might imagine, there are some days when I ask a lot of God. It's OK. I know He can handle it. It's why you've probably heard me say over and over again, "God's got this!" Everything I bring to Him—He's got it covered! It occurs to me that sometimes we might put limits on God. Don't do that! Don't limit Him or place Him in a box by thinking that He can only do what He has done in the past. And another thing. Don't limit God by thinking that He can only meet one need at a time.

The Cross

Tomorrow is Good Friday so I've been thinking a lot about the cross. Being a Christ follower or disciple involves a cross. Carrying a cross, which is what Jesus did, indicates two things: obedience and denying oneself. Dying daily. Submitting my will completely to His. I have to say I don't always succeed at this. Every single day, I have to determine in my heart that what God desires for my life is also what I want. That's easy to say during the good times, isn't it? However, if I truly believe that He is good (I do), and if I truly believe that He loves me (I do), then I should want what He wants and nothing else for my life in both the good times and the bad times.

Why Worry?

Luke 12:25–26 (NIV) says,

> Who of you by worrying can add a single hour to
> his life? Since you cannot do this very little thing,
> why do you worry about the rest?

When you find yourself worrying and feeling anxious, turn to God. You need to get to the place where you can say, "Even though I'm not hearing from God on this matter, even though God hasn't answered the way I want Him to, and even if I don't get what I want, He is still good. He is still trustworthy. He is still faithful. I can trust Him." When you can do that, you'll be free of worry.

Miracles

I'm doing very well. From all appearances, my current treatment program is working. I am so thankful to God for His healing touch. Even though I feel good, I still need a miracle from God if I'm going to beat cancer. Plain and simple. There is no cure for my cancer. If I'm not careful, however, I can focus too much on the miracle I desperately need. The focus should *never* be on the miracle itself but *always* on the miracle worker.

Why Doesn't the Rain Stop?

Recently we took our granddaughter, Madeleine, camping in the motor home at Lake Rudolph and spent several days at Holiday World. When we arrived at our RV site, the hookup to the electricity pedestal was a bit different from at other campgrounds. Most campgrounds have a pedestal to plug the RV's electrical cord into that is about four feet off the ground. This one was only about two feet off the ground. When I hooked up my surge protector to the pedestal and then the RV's electrical cord to the surge protector, the connection was lying on the ground. I didn't give it much thought until we had been there several nights and it rained. It rained so hard it woke me up. After a while, I began to think about this electrical connection lying on the ground. Was it in a hole that might fill with water? Was it even safe to be on the ground as opposed to hanging vertically? I began to pray for the safety of my family and for the motor home. It kept raining and raining, and I worried even more. Then I began to pray that the rain would stop. I prayed that God would cause the storm to blow over. I became more and more upset about the electrical connection and the possible problems that could happen. It kept raining and raining hard. Why wouldn't it just stop raining? I desperately wanted the storm to stop. It didn't. Eventually, I grew tired and fell back to sleep.

When I woke the next morning, the storm had passed and everything in the motor home was fine. When I went out to check on the electric cord, I felt God speaking to me about my frantic prayers the night before. It was as if God said, "It did not matter how long the storm lasted or how much rain fell. What mattered is that I was with you and you made it through the storm." There was no harm to my family and no harm to the motor home. We were protected *through* the storm while I was praying for deliverance *from* the storm. Once again, I understood a valuable lesson. Many times, we want deliverance from the storm, but many times, God wants to deliver us through the storm.

Storms, those difficult seasons of life, push us out of our comfort zones, press us to the edge of ourselves, and often begin to produce fear in us because we are forced to recognize we do not possess the resources to meet our needs! So we pray for deliverance. God! *Please, please, please* get me out of here. But what if the only way to mature in our faith and confidence in God requires that we go through storms? It is much like developing a physical muscle requires putting it under a heavy load/strain. Remember the expression "No pain, no gain." It's true in our walk with Christ as well. What if we recognized that we are as safe in the storm as we are in the sunshine when we stand close to the one who is Lord over both types of weather?

It is impossible for any of us to anticipate the many reasons why God may have us go through storms, but here is what I have learned while living in the midst of my personal cancer storm: Joan and I are closer to God than we have ever been. Our marriage has been strengthened as we find new ways to appreciate each other. I have also grown much closer to friends, family, and coworkers. I have learned much about running to God as my refuge. Sooner or later we all go through difficulties in life. We can take refuge in God and be secure, or we can run from God, blaming Him for the storm.

God Is Always with Me

God is so good. He is so faithful. The Bible tells us that He promises to never leave or forsake us. When you read that or when you hear that, do you really believe it? It's true. You can believe it! He never lies. He never leaves us. He never has and He never will. What an encouragement that is to me today! He is *always* with me. No matter what you are going through today, I pray that you will remember this and be encouraged, knowing that God is always with us.

> When you pass through the waters, I will be with you; and when you pass through the rivers, they will not sweep over you. When you walk through the fire, you will not be burned; the flames will not set you ablaze. (Isaiah 43:2 NIV)

> Even though I walk through the darkest valley, I will fear no evil, for you are with me; your rod and your staff, they comfort me. (Psalm 23:4 NIV)

> The Lord himself goes before you and will be with you; he will never leave you nor forsake you. Do not be afraid; do not be discouraged. (Deuteronomy 31:8)

Heaven

"This must be what heaven feels like." I surprised myself when that statement came out of my mouth. I had been taking prednisone to treat some poison ivy. Prednisone is a powerful anti-inflammatory drug that, in addition to helping with the poison ivy, also took away all of my aches and pains. I had been sitting for a long time on the sofa working with my laptop. When I got up, I suddenly realized that I did not hurt anywhere. That's when I said, without any thought, "This must be what heaven feels like."

We don't talk much about heaven anymore in church. Growing up in Pentecostal churches, we talked a lot about heaven. We sang songs, such as "When We All Get to Heaven" and "I'll Fly Away." We regularly heard sermons on heaven. During Sunday night testimony time, the saints regularly talked about wanting to see Jesus and what they wanted to do when they got to heaven. In hindsight, maybe we were, as some saints used to say, "so heavenly minded we were no earthly good." But there were many reasons why we focused more on heaven back then. Life was not as pleasant for Christians as it is now. We were often ridiculed for our faith in school and at work. People in my church didn't have much money. The world was in the midst of the Cold War. We were reminded once or twice every school year during our air raid drills just how unsafe the world was. Nikita Khrushchev's promise to bury the US and the USSR's buildup of missiles in Cuba were constant reminders that nuclear war was a very real threat. Maybe we dealt with all of the anxiety of our lives by focusing on life hereafter.

It occurs to me, however, that maybe we have swung too far the other way. Do we as Christians even long to see Jesus? Have we become so comfortable here in this life that we are no longer pilgrims in a strange land? Do we see this life as an end to itself or as a tryout for the life hereafter? These thoughts of mine regarding heaven were reinforced recently when I heard Carrie Underwood's song "Temporary Home." The words in the chorus are

> This is my temporary home, it's not where I belong.
> Windows and rooms that I'm passing through.
> This was just a stop on the way to where I'm going.
> I'm not afraid because I know this was my temporary home.
> This is our temporary home.

I think I need to spend more time thinking about the temporal nature of this life. James 4:13–14 (NIV) says,

> Now listen, you who say, Today or tomorrow we will go to this or that city, spend a year there, carry on business and make money. Why, you do not even know what will happen tomorrow. What is your life? You are a mist that appears for a little while and then vanishes.

Get Up!

In 2009, I completed one of the most arduous tasks of my life. I earned a PhD in business administration at the age of fifty-seven. I have done some difficult things in my life but this was by far the most difficult. As I reflect on this accomplishment, some thoughts come to mind regarding why some people succeed and others do not.

Paul Harvey, the radio commentator, is credited with stating the following: If I were ever successful enough that someone was to ask me the secret to my success, I would respond, "Every time I fell down, I got up." That really sums it up nicely, doesn't it? We have all fallen down or been knocked down. Most of us had dreams of how life would turn out, yet life seldom turns out the way we hope. We make plans and then life gets in the way. Troubles come. The road is more difficult than we imagined.

When my granddaughter, Madeleine, was learning how to walk, she fell down a lot. By her first birthday, she was actually walking quite well. Still, sometimes she was just in too big of a hurry. She tripped over her feet. She tripped over her toys. Yet despite all of the falls, she never once seemed to think about staying on the floor. Falling was seemingly just part of the daily routine. She walked some and she fell some. Falling down is not a big deal. Maybe it is even expected.

Assuming that Madeleine is not all that different from most kids, I have to wonder when it was that we, as humans, quit believing that falling down is part of life. Why do we believe that life will not include some falling down? Why do we get so upset when things aren't perfect? Why do we expect life to be easy?

Successful people have apparently determined that failure is not terminal. Maybe you remember the stories of great people who suffered tremendous setbacks in their life. George Washington was a failure as a young military leader. Abe Lincoln suffered several political disappointments in his career. Remember Thomas Edison's attempts at finding the right filament for the incandescent light bulb? Edison said that his failed attempts at finding the right filament were actually successful attempts at finding what would *not* work.

Winston Churchill was repeatedly rejected by the people of Great Britain before becoming prime minister. Maybe those personal failures were responsible for his oft quoted speech from 1941 in which he said,

> Never give in, never, never, never, never—in nothing great or small, large or petty—never give in except to convictions of honor and good sense. Never yield to force; never yield to the apparently overwhelming might of the enemy.

The Bible certainly has a lot to say about failures. Joseph ended up in prison for honoring his moral convictions. Noah was ridiculed for his boat-building efforts. David committed despicable personal failures in judgment in front of his entire nation. Peter lied about knowing Jesus. In 2 Corinthians 11:24–26 (NIV), Paul writes,

> Five times I received from the Jews the forty lashes minus one. Three times I was beaten with rods, once I was stoned, three times I was shipwrecked, I spent a night and a day in the open sea, I have

been constantly on the move. I have been in danger from rivers, in danger from bandits, in danger from my own countrymen, in danger from Gentiles; in danger in the city, in danger in the country, in danger at sea; and in danger from false brothers.

Don't misunderstand. We all want to give up at some point. We have all asked if it is worth it. The difference is that some give up easily and some fight on. Seek God's will for your life, and if you believe He is leading you in a particular direction, then fight on. You will be knocked down and you will struggle. Learn from your struggles and keep going. Get up and get on with what God has for your life.

Salvation

Today as I was receiving my chemotherapy, I realized two things. First, it dawned on me that it has been two years since I was diagnosed with cancer. Two *years* since I was essentially told that I might only have two *months* to live. To God be the glory! Second, I began to notice that the order of the medications being given to me never changes. The nurse explained that it is very important to give each of the IV medications in a very specific order every single time. If that doesn't happen, the chemo might not be as effective or I might have more side effects. That is very important indeed. But do you know what is even more important? Your relationship with Jesus Christ. That is the most important thing you will ever have. When that relationship is nailed down, you can weather any storm—even cancer. If you haven't already done so, I pray that you will surrender your life to Him today. I promise you it will be the best decision you ever make.

Short-Term versus Long-Term Thinking

I just finished my workout routine. I feel great. I'm tired and a little sore, but I feel great. An hour ago, I did not feel so well. I was tired. I was sore. I did not want to work out. I had plenty of reasons for not wanting to work out today. I had already worked out plenty of times this week. I just didn't feel like working out. I didn't have a lot of time to work out before I had to get ready and go out. How many reasons does a person need for not wanting to work out? But I did work out, and now I feel better than I did before. I knew I needed to work out, but I nearly let my feelings overcome what I knew to be the right thing to do. Many things in life are like that. I have arthritis. One of the doctor-recommended ways to reduce the pain and stiffness of arthritis is to exercise. But exercise hurts. What's the sense in that? Yet every time I exercise, the arthritis hurts less.

Many times, our feelings can get us into trouble. We know what is right, but we don't feel like doing what is right. I don't feel like exercising so I don't. Then I feel less like exercising the next time so I don't. Eventually I never feel like it so I never exercise again. Why should we exercise? Why should we eat right? Why shouldn't we give in to what feels good at the time? We know the answer. Because long-term it is best for us.

Mathew 16:24–26 (NIV) says,

> Then Jesus said to his disciples, If anyone would come after me, he must deny himself and take up his cross and follow me. For whoever wants to save his life will lose it, but whoever loses his life for me will find it. What good will it be for a man if he gains the whole world, yet forfeits his soul? Or what can a man give in exchange for his soul?

Take up a cross? Deny myself? Why should I do that? Lose my life? Why? Because long term (and short term), it's best. People who take a "long-term thinking" approach to life are the ones who are best able to overcome their feelings and make the correct choices in life. If I think short term, I stay on the couch and don't exercise. If I think long term, I realize that a little pain now pays off. Long-term thinking means I save money today so that I have a retirement fund and a rainy-day fund in the future. Short-term thinking allows me to spend every dime I have on my wants now. People who take a long-term view of life prepare themselves by going to college, learning a trade, or just learning new skills. Short-term thinkers don't worry about tomorrow.

Really long-term thinkers consider where they will spend eternity and prepare themselves now to meet God one day. Short-term thinkers don't want to think that far ahead.

What are you thinking about? Are you thinking long term or short term?

Mercy and Grace

Merry Christmas. Take a moment and think about Christmases past. What are the various reactions you have had in response to Christmas gifts? God has offered us a gift. Gifts are not earned. We cannot earn our way to God. In order to give a gift to someone, the giver generally has to purchase it. Our gift from God was purchased on Calvary with the death of Jesus. This gift is available to those who believe and accept Christ as Savior. This is such a great picture of mercy and grace. My sin earned me death. Someone had to die for my sin. It seems only logical that it should be me. But I will not receive the wages of my sin. We call that God's mercy. Instead, Christ paid my debt of death on Calvary and has given me the gift of life. I get eternal life, which I do not deserve; we call that God's grace. A simple way of evaluating our understanding of God's mercy and grace is to measure how much of a sacrifice of our lives we are making. The amount of our sacrifice is a reflection of how much we understand and appreciate God's mercy.

Butterfly Effect

According to Answers.com,

In 1961, Edward Lorenz was using a numerical computer model to rerun a weather prediction, when, as a shortcut on a number in the sequence, he entered the decimal .506 instead of entering the full .506127. The result was a completely different weather scenario. Lorenz published his findings in a 1963 paper for the New York Academy of Sciences noting that "One meteorologist remarked that if the theory were correct, one flap of a seagull's wings could change the course of weather forever." Later speeches and papers by Lorenz used the more poetic butterfly. According to Lorenz, upon failing to provide a title for a talk he was to present at the 139th meeting of the American Association for the Advancement of Science in 1972, Philip Merilees concocted, "Does the flap of a butterfly's wings in Brazil set off a tornado in Texas?" as a title (http://www. answers.com/topic/butterfly-effect-2).

The Butterfly Effect postulates that an insignificant event on one side of the world can produce significant change in the outcome of events on the other side of the world. Can this be possible?

What about the bit players in the Bible? We study the great men and women, but what about the supporting cast? What about those who played seemingly insignificant roles? The apostle Andrew is recorded in John with bringing his brother Peter to Christ. Peter became a great leader in the early church. A boy gave away his lunch that led to over 5,000 being fed when Christ blessed it.

Prior to teaching full time for Indiana Wesleyan University, I was a faculty recruiter. Since IWU wants to hire faculty who can support its Christ-centered mission, I would always ask prospective faculty to tell me about their walk with Christ. Roughly half of those who could articulate a personal relationship with Christ said that they were raised in church all of their lives and then one day, they accepted Christ as Savior. The other half would tell me about a journey they experienced with different people in their lives pointing them toward Jesus until one day they came face-to-face with their need of a Savior and accepted Christ.

I loved listening to these stories. One in particular went like this: This young man (let's call him George) and his wife met another couple who were much like themselves. George and his wife were invited to attend a Sunday school class social event. There they met other couples like themselves and really enjoyed the evening. When George and his wife were invited to attend the Sunday school class, they accepted and then they attended church as well on a regular basis. A short time later, George and his wife moved away and quit going to church. Years later, George was handed a New Testament by a Gideon. George tossed the book in his book bag and forgot about it. Several weeks later, George was called to visit his dad's bedside who was dying in another state. George was leaving to return home and began thinking about his dad dying and his mother and sister fending for themselves. It saddened him to think that he and his dad had not resolved the issues between them. George started rummaging through his book bag and found the New Testament. He flipped through it and eventually started reading 1 Corinthians 13, the love chapter. The Word spoke to him. He saw the answers to many of life's problems. When his plane landed, he excitedly told his wife that he had figured out the answer to his problems. The answer he said was love. His wife, who had not shared in this epiphany, replied, "No kidding."

George did not know that his wife had been attending a Bible study at a neighbor's house. God had been speaking to his wife, but she wasn't ready to discuss what God had been doing in her life. Over the next several weeks, the masks came off and George and his wife realized that God had been speaking to each of them and it was time to get back to church and make a commitment to God.

I share all of this—the butterfly effect and George's story—to encourage each of us to make that effort to point someone to Christ. Even just a little nudge can make an impact. We never know the impact of our actions.

Matthew 10:41–42 (NIV) tells us,

> Anyone who receives a prophet because he is a prophet will receive a prophet's reward, and anyone who receives a righteous man because he is a righteous man will receive a righteous man's reward. And if anyone gives even a cup of cold water to one of these little ones because he is my disciple, I tell you the truth, he will certainly not lose his reward.

First Corinthians 3:7–9 (NIV) says,

> So neither he who plants nor he who waters is anything, but only God, who makes things grow. The man who plants and the man who waters have one purpose, and each will be rewarded according to his own labor. For we are God's fellow workers; you are God's field, God's building.

God Uses Flawed People

On chemo day, I spend approximately five hours at the cancer center. I use the time I am there to grade papers and read my Bible. I love reading the Old Testament stories in the Bible about the people that God used. They were flawed just like me. Abraham had difficulty trusting God, so he lied to protect himself. Then later he decided to "help" God provide him with the son God had promised him. King David, whom Paul described as "a man after God's own heart," committed adultery and then killed an innocent man in order to try to cover up his transgression. I take comfort in the fact that God uses flawed, broken individuals like me.

Why Do You Follow Christ?

Someone recently asked me, "What would you say to someone questioning their faith due to their circumstances?" First of all, let me say that I want to avoid sounding trite. Trite answers don't work for those of us who are suffering. The simple answer is that we live in an imperfect world. Imagine two workers up on a scaffolding; one is a Christian and one is not. The scaffolding gives way. Gravity takes over and both workers fall to the ground and are seriously injured. Gravity is no respecter of persons any more than cancer, ALS, or many other difficulties in life. You may ask, "Why should I serve God if He is going to allow horrible things to happen to me just like everyone else in the world?" If that ultimately is your question, then I have to ask you why you are following Christ in the first place. If it were to escape hell or because you thought you would have a better life here on earth, you picked the wrong reason. You picked a reason that only serves you, not God. If you were following Christ in response to His mercy, grace, and love, then I have to ask, "What changed?" Jesus never promised us an easy life. In fact, He promised His followers that they would be persecuted.

Faith Walk

Our faith in God must include the belief that God is good and we are loved by Him. He is good based on His definition of good, not ours. Sometimes I think we try to judge God based on a very incomplete view of the world and eternity. We judge God primarily on our self-centeredness and what we believe is important. Many times, we don't even think about what God considers to be important. We try to make sense of this world based on our incomplete view and comprehension. Faith is built on a relationship with God. We learn to trust Him only after we have spent significant time with Him. This walk of ours is a faith walk. I pray that you never forget this: God cannot love you any more than He already does, and He will not love you any less than He already does.

A Trustworthy God

I have undergone a lot of tests this month. I have had a PET scan, a CT scan, and even a liver biopsy. These tests will give my physicians greater insight into what type of treatment is now needed since it appears that the cancer has returned. With all the appointments being scheduled, it would be easy to just get overwhelmed with worry, fear, and doubt. Instead, I choose to remain in God's Word. I love the scriptures! They remind me time and time again that God is so trustworthy, even when the circumstances swirling around me are cause for concern. Joan says that when she feels herself getting overwhelmed or worried, she just repeats the simple phrase "I trust You, Lord. I trust You, Lord. I trust You, Lord." I remember an old hymn we used to sing in the little country church I attended many years ago. It is called, "He's as Close as the Mention of His Name." I'm so thankful for that.

Trusting God

The following is copied from Joan's journal.

> Bill saw the oncologist today. His CT scan, PET scan, and liver biopsy results are in. And they are not good. The cancer has definitely returned in both the esophagus and throughout the liver. Starting tomorrow morning, he will go back on the Oxaliplatin (nasty drug) that he was on when he was first diagnosed two and a half years ago. Hopefully, it will work as well as it did previously. If not, then he will be started on a different drug/chemo. While this is certainly not what we had hoped or prayed for, we know that none of this has taken the Lord by surprise. God is good, even when test results are not. We have done all that we can do, and now we need to trust God. The battle is His, not ours. Cancer must bow to the name of Jesus!

Trusting God? What does that look like? Especially now that my cancer has returned. It occurred to me recently as I was considering what it means to have trust in God that my trust is not that He will produce a desired outcome. My trust is that He will take care of me.

I hope and pray that He sees fit to heal me soon. But fortunately, my hope in God extends far beyond this life. As Paul said in 1 Corinthians 15:19 (NIV), "If only for this life we have hope in Christ, we are to be pitied more than all men." Paul's life was filled with difficulties, but his hope was in eternity. Because of this hope in eternal life, we can discuss plans to leave this life with a great deal of peace, knowing that for the Christian, things will turn out for our best. God's got this!

When Trouble Comes
(A.K.A. When
Cancer Returns)

Five major points:

1. God always knows what is going on. We may be surprised when we lose our jobs or get a diagnosis of cancer, but God is never surprised.
2. God always has a plan. Because He is never surprised, He has figured out how to use tragedies in our lives for His purposes.
3. God's plans always encompass reality. Our plans never include losing our jobs or getting cancer, which is my reality. Our plans are based on everything always going perfectly, which is *not* reality. God's plans include the tragedies that happen as part of living in this messed-up world.
4. God's plans always encompass eternity. Our plans seldom encompass eternity, but that is always God's main objective. God always takes the long-term, eternal view.
5. We seldom comprehend God's plan. Because we can only see what is in front of us, we seldom comprehend what God is trying to accomplish with His plan. Like people watching

a long parade through a knothole in a fence, we fail to see and comprehend God's big picture.

During my cancer journey, many people have been praying for me. One of the important things I have learned about praying for someone is that it is way more effective when you regularly let that person know you are praying for them. Many times, at just the right time, I'll get a text message or email from someone with just the words "I'm still praying for you." You have no idea how encouraging that is to me.

Hearing from God

In John 10:3–5 (NIV), Jesus said,

> The watchman opens the gate for him, and the sheep listen to his voice. He calls his own sheep by name and leads them out. When he has brought out all his own, he goes on ahead of them, and his sheep follow him because they know his voice. But they will never follow a stranger; in fact, they will run away from him because they do not recognize a stranger's voice.

We learn to recognize the voice of God when we spend time—lots of time—with Him. He speaks through His Word. He speaks in our quiet times of meditation and reflection. He speaks through godly teaching, preaching, and music. When God speaks to me, it is generally through scripture or song. If those scriptures and songs were not part of my mind, then I'm not sure I would hear from God. I'd like to challenge you today to get serious about the amount of time spent on activities that can help us to renew our minds and become more like Christ. We can't possibly counteract hours and hours of television, Facebook, and movie time with a seventy-five-minute church service once a week. We have to be deliberate and intentional about spending time with God.

Waiting on God

This morning, Joan and I were talking about being more intentional in our walk with Christ, looking for ways to share our testimonies for all that God is doing in and through us on this cancer journey. There are so many things I still want to do for God. Because of my cancer, it is difficult sometimes for me to understand what I should be doing for the kingdom. It is difficult to know how to plan. It is difficult to even know what God wants me to do. I asked Joan, "Wouldn't it be great if one day I just woke up and found a note from God saying, 'Bill, I heard you and here's what I want you to do … Here's what I have planned for you … Here's where I want you to serve'?" That would be so cool, wouldn't it? I'm sorry, but it doesn't happen that way. We have to wait on His timing. Wait for Him to open a door. Wait for His guidance. And while we wait, we serve as best we can, wherever we can, for whomever we can, for as long as we can.

Worship

I love worship! There's just something so amazing about singing praises to God with my hands lifted toward the heavens. Worship or singing praises to God isn't just something that happens on Sunday mornings at church. Worship is how we live every day, all day. Worship is me declaring that God is with me through this cancer journey. He is with me at every chemo visit. He is with me at every CT scan. Regardless of what is happening in the world around me, I know that He is with me. I choose to worship God in spite of my circumstances. I choose to surrender my will to His will. Joan says that when she worships Jesus, she has a picture in her mind of Satan getting all kinds of frustrated and annoyed and needing to leave. How will you choose to worship God this week?

The Alpha and Omega

Recently, a nice lady at church stopped me and asked how she could be free of worry. She said, "I pray to God to help me with worrying, but I don't see any answers, and this causes even more anxiety and worry." She felt that she was trusting God, but she still worried a lot. I shared with her that our trust has to be in *Him,* not the outcome we are asking for and not necessarily what we want to happen or what we think needs to happen. Worry is actually the opposite of trust. Worship is worry in reverse. My wife likes to joke and say that she used to be a world-class worrier. Now she is a world-class worshipper! Just because we pray and God hasn't answered should not be a reason to worry. We pray. We give the situation to Him. We trust that He will do what is best. That's called walking by faith. We trust Him, even when we don't receive an answer. We trust Him, even when He is silent. It's the only way to have peace about our problems. Once you give it to Him and trust Him to handle it, you can be at peace (free of worry). God doesn't want us all tied up with worry, anxieties, etc. Again, our trust must always be in Him, not in the outcome we are seeking. Our trust must always be in only Him. Trusting that He knows what is best. He has it all figured out. He is the King of kings and Lord of lords, the Alpha and Omega, the beginning and the end, the first and the last. We can put our faith, hope, and trust in Him because He knows what is best. He really does. He has it all figured out.

God's got this!

Three Years since Being Told I Had Three Months to Live

We saw the oncologist at MD Anderson this morning for results of yesterday's PET scan. The scan shows that everything is very stable. On the one hand, we would like to have seen that the lesions in the esophagus and liver were gone or at least shrinking. On the other hand, it could be so much worse, possibly even spreading to other organs. That is *not* the case, and we thank the Lord that things are stable. The oncologist was able to get us an appointment to see a radiation oncologist today (thank You, Lord). She feels that while radiation may not have been a treatment option three years ago, it is definitely an option now. She has made the recommendations for radiation therapy and we are hoping and praying that I can receive it in Fort Myers. Thank you for praying with us on this journey. We have felt *every single prayer!*

Thought for the day: Your greatest victory, the answer to your prayer, may very well come after your darkest night. *Never* stop praying!

Patience

Proverbs 14:29 (NIV) says, "A patient man has great understanding, but a quick-tempered man displays folly."

Proverbs 19:11 (NIV) says, "A man's wisdom gives him patience; it is to his glory to overlook an offense."

I have an application on my phone that downloads a daily scripture reading. Several days ago, I read these verses. When I read them, I had to stop and think. My first reaction was that my father had never read these verses. I laughed about that for a while. (He was a very impatient man.)

But then I had to think about me. How do these apply to me? I like to think I have a great deal of wisdom and understanding. I like to think that I am not foolish. The question, of course, is this: do I display patience? Sometimes, I do. Unfortunately, many times I do not.

When I am driving and I see someone tailgating me on a two-lane road, I have started pulling over when I can to let them get to where they want to go in such a hurry. That to me is a sign of understanding. I'm displaying patience. I will let someone in line ahead of me in traffic sometimes. I'll laugh to myself at the people who cut in front of me in a line, sometimes patiently and quietly waiting.

But most people who know me would probably say that is not the whole story. Sometimes I am that person doing the tailgating.

Sometimes I am rude to people who are not ready to pay the cashier after waiting in line forever. Sometimes I am impatient. Why does Solomon equate patience with wisdom and understanding? Why doesn't he blame it on bad genes? Why doesn't he say it's just the way a person is and they can't help it? I guess Solomon observed that impatience is a problem with a lack of wisdom and/or understanding.

If I understand that sometimes I'm the one who forgets to have my payment handy when I'm checking out, then maybe I'll be a little more patient when I see someone else do it. If I understand that the old man who is poking along in front of me will be me someday, then maybe I can muster up some patience. If I understand that with all my rushing around impatiently I may be missing an opportunity for God to speak to me, then maybe I can slow down and patiently accept what God wants to teach me today. If I understand that it was only the Good Samaritan who took the time to minister to the man in need, I might patiently look around to see where God would want me to minister today.

How about the part that says, "It is to his glory to overlook an offense"? That's what God did for me. He could have demanded that I pay for my sins with my blood. How many times have I offended Him?

Ouch. This hurts, and I don't like it one bit. Lord, help me to live patiently today. Help me to understand that nothing will happen to me today that You are not aware of. Help me to understand that You may have some work for me today that requires to me to patiently wait in a line or patiently stop to minister. Help me to remember that You have overlooked my offenses and I should be happy to overlook the offenses of others. Help me to patiently wait on You for guidance today.

A Living Sacrifice

Merry Christmas!

What does a living sacrifice look like for us in America? I'm pretty sure it does not look like "I'll go to church when I feel like it." It does not look like "I don't have any money left over for God this month. I'll get Him next month." It does not look like "God, You want me to do what?" A living sacrifice means I look more and more like Christ and less and less like me. A living sacrifice looks like being a servant or slave to God. It means total surrender of my life, my desires, and my will to His. So what are we to do? I'll be the first to admit I don't have this all figured out. But here's the thing: Are we at least moving in that direction? In some cases, it may take some time to arrange our lives to be in total submission to God's will. I understand that and I believe that God understands that we cannot make major changes to our lives overnight. The more obligations we currently have, the longer it may take to become totally submitted to Christ in all aspects of our life. Are we freeing up more money to give to God's work? Are we freeing up more time in our lives to spend in His Word and His work? Are we listening to the Holy Spirit when He tells us to fix an area of our lives?

Closer to God

I've noticed that the further from God I am, the more I fool myself into believing that God and I are OK. During these times, I find the freedom to do things that I would not do when I am closer to God. I talk of God's mercy and how I have sinned. My church attendance, Bible reading, and prayer times become more "optional" as I begin to rely on the past to get me through the present. Conversely, the closer to God I am, the more I see how much I need Him. I desire to spend more time in church, Bible reading, and prayer. I find myself wanting to spend more time in His presence. I begin to see myself as less and less perfect as I strive for His holiness. I desire to rid my life of things that are displeasing to God. How close are you to God?

I Have Decided to Follow Jesus

Today is my last chemo treatment in Florida, at least for a while. When I am finished here in a few hours, Joan and I are headed to Houston, Texas, for the next few months. The motor home is all packed up and we are ready to move out. It appears that the radiation therapy and my current chemotherapy regimen are no longer working. I have been accepted into a clinical trial at MD Anderson Cancer Center in Houston. I pray that this new treatment works. As I'm sitting here in the chemo chair, I'm remembering the promise of God that there is coming a day when the Lord shall wipe every tear from our eyes. There will be no more pain. No more sorrow. No more night.

When I was a teenager, there was a popular song that my church sang quite often. The lyrics are as follows:

I have decided to follow Jesus; I have decided to follow Jesus.

I have decided to follow Jesus, No turning back, no turning back.

My favorite verse went like this:

The world behind me, the Cross before me; The world behind me, the Cross before me.

The world behind me, the Cross before me; No turning back, no turning back.

Always Faithful

We arrived in Houston a few weeks ago. Shortly after our arrival, the coronavirus pandemic hit. We are safe and secure in our motor home. MD Anderson Cancer Center is amazing, and so is our God!

God is faithful in everything—finances, relationships, health issues, and whatever other type of problem you are facing. God is the answer. He was the answer in the past, He is the answer today, and He will be the answer in the future. No matter the circumstances. No matter how big or how bad the problem is. God is *always* faithful.

Sometimes people ask me, "Have you ever asked God why you got cancer?" The answer is no. Not because I'm some sort of super Christian. It's because I had this settled prior to my diagnosis. As I've said many times, it's during the good times that we need to nail down what we believe. We like to search for answers. If there is a reason for our suffering, then we think we can handle it better. The truth is we may never know the reasons why. If God believes it is important, then He may reveal a reason for my cancer through the Holy Spirit. Because we only see what is in front of us, we seldom comprehend what God is trying to accomplish with His plan. For those who are Christ followers, He is there at the end of this life opening the door to a better, eternal life.

I'm Still Learning

A friend recently asked me, "What has God taught you during this experience?" While there are many things I could list, four things immediately come to mind.

1. There is a saying in the cancer community that says, "No one makes it through cancer alone." God desires us to be dependent on each other. There are tremendous blessings available by giving up some independence in order to allow others to minister to us. We get blessed, and others who are allowed to minister to us also get blessed.

2. We are all equal when it comes to cancer and the other difficulties in life. I see old and young, wealthy and poor, and people of all colors in the Infusion Clinic. It's a snapshot of our broken world. We are all equally broken and in need. If the rich man's money would save him, Steve Jobs would still be alive.

3. Cancer reminds me of sin. I want it out of my body. I don't want to be *mostly* cancer free. I want to be *totally* free of cancer. Sin consumes all it possesses like an untreated cancer. Don't allow a little bit of sin in your life any more than you would be happy with a little bit of cancer growing inside you.

4. We must always remember this: God is good. God loves His children. He is faithful. Get as close to Him as you can in the good times, and hold on tightly in the bad times.

Five Precepts for Understanding the Difficulties or Storms of Life

1. God always has a plan. *Always.* When I was diagnosed with cancer, I was completely caught off guard. God wasn't though. He wasn't caught off guard, and He wasn't surprised or shocked. You see, He had a plan. The scriptures tell us that God is a strategic planner. Way back in the Garden of Eden, God had a plan. Adam and Eve sinned and rebelled against God. God shared with them His plan—just a glimpse of it. He didn't give them a lot of details, but He revealed to them that He had a plan for man's redemption. Thousands of years before Christ would ever walk this earth, God already had a plan for how to fix this problem of sin in the world. God always has a plan. Joan and I have prayed a lot and continue to pray a lot regarding this cancer diagnosis. God has spoken to us both many times concerning this cancer situation. Do you know what? He's never once said, "Man, I'm really sorry about this. I really dropped the ball on this." Not once has He said, "I don't really know how you got this

cancer. I just don't know how it happened." Instead, He has assured us that He is in control. He has assured us that it will be OK. He has assured us that He has a plan and He is in charge of the plan. He is working things out according to His plan. You see, this cancer diagnosis is not some random act of the universe. It's not a mistake. It's not some bizarre thing that just somehow happened to me. It's all part of a plan. I can take comfort in knowing that it is all part of a plan—and that God is going to do something with it.

2. God is good. This cancer journey I'm walking through has shown me just how good God really is. God is good in spite of our circumstances. It's easy to walk out of the doctor's office when you get good news and say, "God is good!" Or when you get that raise or that promotion at work, it's easy to say, "God is good!" For the first two and a half years of my cancer journey, almost all the news we received from the scans and lab results was good. It was easy to walk out of the doctor's office and say, "God is good." Starting in April 2019, however, we started getting bad news. And we have seen a lot of bad news since then. This month has been especially difficult. It would appear that this treatment I am receiving is not having the effect we had hoped for. God has made it very clear to me, however, that I can't say, "He is good," only when I like what is happening in my life. He made it very clear to me that I can't say, "He is good," only when I'm getting good news and then stop saying it when I get bad news. The reason is because God doesn't change. He is good. It's His nature. It's who He is. I'll be very honest with you. This is hard to accept sometimes. I don't see anything good about having cancer. I have seen some good things come from it, but I still don't think it's all that great. I'm not saying that God isn't good, I'm just saying I can't see it all the time. I'm human. I can only see what's right in front of me. I can't see into the future. I can't see what's

going on in other people's lives. I don't see anything good about cancer, but I have never doubted for one minute that God is good. This is where faith comes in. I accept, by faith, that God is working all things for good in my life. God has some good purpose in this plan, and I'll probably never fully understand it. And that's OK. Because God is good and He is good all the time. Not most of the time. Not some of the time. Not nine out of ten times. Not ninety-nine out of one hundred times. He is *always* good.

3. God is sovereign. The day that God scooped up a handful of dirt, shaped it into a man, and breathed life into it, God had the authority to rule over humankind. The psalmist said, "He's our creator." We didn't create Him. He's not a figment of our imagination. No. He made us. And as our creator, He has the divine right to do His sovereign work the way He sees fit. In His divine and sovereign will, He allowed this cancer to come into my life. I have to believe that He OK'd it. I have to believe that He approved it because I believe that He is omniscient; He is all-knowing. I believe that He is omnipresent; He is everywhere all at the same time. I believe that He is omnipotent; He is all-powerful. I have seen times when God has prevented bad things from happening to me. I have seen Him supernaturally intervene on my behalf. This time, however, He didn't. I don't believe for one minute that God gave me cancer or that He somehow caused me to have the cancer. I do believe that He allowed it to grow in my body. Unfortunately, we live in a broken and sinful world, which is far different from the world God created. In His sovereignty, God decided that I would go through this trial, this storm. He OK'd it, and I'm OK with that.

When we pray to God, I believe that He will sovereignly do one of three things:

- Sometimes God answers our prayers very quickly. My mom had a tumor on her intestines and before the surgeon could even operate on it, the tumor was gone! It was there, and then it wasn't there. God very quickly answered our prayers that time.
- Sometimes God says, "No. What you are asking Me for is not in My divine will. It is not what I want for you."
- Sometimes God says, "Not now." He may say, "You're going to struggle for a while. You're going to go through this difficult time." If He decides that to be the case, then that's just the way it is.

Many times, we don't understand why God does what He does. We may not understand why He healed someone right away and then He chose to not heal someone else. That's OK. God's got it. I know that I'm not going through this because of something I did or didn't do. It's just part of God's plan. And it's a good plan. In God's sovereign will, He will do it the way He desires to have it done.

4. God will never leave us or forsake us. We find these words in the book of Hebrews, and they are actually a repeat of what God told Joshua in the Old Testament. We see God frequently telling Joshua to not be afraid. That's good because frequently I get afraid and frequently you get afraid too. Since I received my cancer diagnosis, God has taught Joan and me this in ways that are just amazing. Every now and then, He just says or does something to prove to us that He is walking with us and many times even ahead of us, opening up doors that we need to walk through and closing doors that we don't need to be walking through, to make this journey a little better for us. It's part of His plan and His plan is good. He is sovereign, and He never leaves us or forsakes us.

5. The reason why we may go through difficult times doesn't really matter. We can spend an inordinate amount of time trying to figure it out, trying to understand why God is doing this and what His plan is. All of it is just a waste of time. If I accept that God has a plan and I accept that God is good, then I've learned to accept that that is good enough. The why just isn't important to me. I don't know why I have cancer. There's no answer that seems good enough. I can't see what God sees. Isaiah tells us that His ways are so far above our ways. It's like the sky over the earth. It's only in our suffering and in our lack of resources that God is able to reveal Himself to us. I think just maybe that's the only reason why. When we become totally dependent on God for health, finances, a job, food, relationships, etc., then He can reveal himself to be Jehovah Jireh, the God who provides. As long as we are leaning on our own resources and on our own abilities, God can't reveal Himself to us. We can't comprehend it until we've experienced total dependence on Him. I have to believe that many times that alone is the reason for the storm. It's not important that I consume myself trying to understand the reason. Instead, my focus and your focus need to be on the revelation. What is it that God is trying to show me through this?

Christians Don't Die

Christians don't die. Have you ever thought about that or realized that? We never die. When it's all over, it's not really over. We just relocate to a better place. Pastor Greg Laurie says it this way: "Easter was the death of death." When I take my last breath on this earth, my very next breath will be in the presence of Jesus.

> Jesus said to her, I am the resurrection and the life. He who believes in me will live, even though he dies; and whoever lives and believes in me will never die. (John 11:25–26 NIV)

Epilogue

By Joan Burton

Bill lost his battle with cancer on July 2, 2020. His funeral was so beautiful. I loved that we were able to make it truly a celebration of his life. Naturally, I loved seeing so many family members, friends, and coworkers of Bill's. I loved hearing all the wonderful things being said about him. On the evening after the funeral, I found myself wanting to talk to him about it all. The way we used to do after leaving a party or an event. So I did. And I felt better. I am deeply sad that he is gone and my heart is broken. But I know he has received his crown of life. Bill died with the certain hope of eternal life and is now made whole again. Bill's life simply overflowed with Jesus's love. I *know* I will see him again. I saw something on Facebook several years ago and can't remember who said it, but I thought about it again recently. This morning, I'd like to ask Satan, "So how's that crushed skull feeling?" Bill won. You lost, Satan.

Although many wonderful things were shared about him during his funeral service, there are still some things that I would like to share. These are things that I wish I could have shared during the funeral, but I know my emotions simply would not have allowed me to do so. I pray that you will also see this as my testimony of God's faithfulness during a very dark time in my life. The day cancer showed up in my husband's life, God showed up even bigger in my life.

There are some days when I still find it so hard to believe Bill is really gone. I try to keep busy with work and other activities, but at the end of the day, he's still not here and I miss him terribly. I do allow myself to grieve. I cry (a lot!) because my heart is broken. However, I don't dwell in my grief. After a few minutes, I stop and shift my focus on the many blessings that God has given me. I have found that it is virtually impossible to be sad when I am praising the King of kings! God is always good. He never makes a mistake. He is so worthy of our praise.

As it relates to Bill's passing, I'll share just a few of the things for which I will forever be grateful to the Lord.

- When Bill was first diagnosed with cancer in October 2016, he was given only two to three months to live. But we had nearly four years together! For at least two of those years, he was completely free of disease and felt great! In fact, it really wasn't until approximately January 2020 that he began feeling poor. We squeezed a lot of travel and fun into the forty-five months we had together *after* receiving the cancer diagnosis. Thank You, Lord.

- We made it back to Indiana from Texas in June 2020. It took four days of Bill driving the RV, and although he was getting weaker with each mile, we made it home! Thank You, Lord.

- Bill spent six days at Parkview Hospital at the end of June, four of which were in the intensive care unit. I couldn't be with him due to the COVID-19 pandemic. I will always be grateful that he didn't pass away in the hospital, alone or with strangers. Thank You, Lord.

- Bill was able to move into our beautiful new house. Although he only spent three nights in it before he passed away, it made him so happy just to know that I would be settled, secure, and safe. The night before he passed away, he sat in his recliner and said, "I see lots of ladies' Bible studies happening here." He knew my heart. Thank You, Lord.

- Although his last day was difficult and I know he was uncomfortable, with the help of the Lord, Pastor Duane, Pastor Steve, Kerri, and the hospice nurses, I really feel like we did a great job of taking care of most of his pain. It was still only one day. It could have been so much worse. I'm so thankful he didn't suffer very much or for very long. Thank You, Lord.

- Perhaps the most precious thing of all that I am grateful for is the way Bill passed. He had been sleeping most of the day and evening due to the morphine he required for pain. However, just after midnight, he looked me straight in the eye and—I swear—into my soul, and in a very clear voice he said, "Bye, bye." With Kerri and me at his bedside, holding his hand and kissing his face, he turned his head, looked over to the doorway, and smiled. There was no one in the doorway—at least that we could see. Then once again, he very peacefully said, "Bye, bye," and then he was gone. Thank You, Lord.

In the days since his graduation to heaven, I have enjoyed reading from Bill's prayer journal and sermon notes. They have brought me so much joy and comfort! I rejoice just knowing that he is free of cancer, completely healed, and whole. I rejoice knowing that I will see him again in heaven, where we will spend eternity together with our Lord!

Bill lived a life that showed how much he loved the Lord. He loved sharing his faith with others. Yes, he was an engineer. He was a businessman. He was an assistant professor. He was a financial advisor and coach. But he was also an encourager, mentor, and friend to so many. He loved golf, traveling in the RV, photography, and politics. He was a voracious reader. He was a wonderful husband, dad, and pop-pop. He was loved by so many. He never missed a day of not only telling me but, more importantly, showing me just how much he loved me. He truly was my best friend. Even though his last few days on this earth were uncomfortable for him, he still read from God's Word every day. On the last day, when he simply did not have the strength to do so, he asked me to read certain scriptures for him. He would say, "Read 2 Timothy 4:6–8 to me. Read Psalm 18:1–6. Read John 14:1–6. Read Revelation 21:3–5. He knew all of these scriptures by heart, and quite remarkably, he knew where they could be found in God's Word.

Bill's cancer journey was difficult, but God was with us through it all. Every single day, God let us know that we were on His mind. He reminded us time and time again that He would never leave us. We felt the sweet presence of the Holy Spirit in ways that we had never felt before. God showed us that despite our circumstances, we could put our faith, hope, and trust in Him. While I wouldn't wish my loss on anyone, I do wish each of you could experience the depth of love and peace that our Lord has provided to me every single day since Bill passed away.

I want to also thank everyone who prayed for Bill and me from the day we first learned of his cancer diagnosis. As you can imagine, it was quite shocking and completely unexpected. Our friends and family came alongside us in those early days and over the next four years, lifting us up in prayer on an ongoing basis. Bill appreciated your prayers so much and regularly commented on how special not only our real family was but also the "family of God" who was lifting us up in prayer. I know it's a cliché, but truly the cards, emails, and text messages always seemed to come at just the right time, and they were always a wonderful source of encouragement to us. Thank you.

You prayed with us that God would perform a miracle. While I still mourn that we didn't get the miracle we all hoped for here on this earth, there were so many other miracles that we witnessed throughout the nearly four-year period of time that Bill had cancer. I know that Bill is completely healed and is more alive now than he ever was here on earth. Bill gave me so many wonderful memories in our nearly thirty-five years of married life.

Bill loved to "preach" whenever he had the opportunity to do so. He was very comfortable with public speaking, whether it was teaching students as an assistant professor at Indiana Wesleyan University, teaching a small group, leading a Bible study, or preaching at our church. Bill also enjoyed writing his blog about his journey with cancer. He wanted to share with others all that God was doing in his life, despite cancer, despite chemotherapy, and despite all the doctor visits. Bill was still teaching full time for Indiana Wesleyan University in its online degree programs until about one week before he passed away. I remember one night when he called me from his bed in the intensive care unit at the hospital, where he was being treated for blood clots in both lungs and a bleeding esophageal tumor. He said, "Well, I was thinking maybe you should call my boss and ask him to take over my classes until I can get home and get feeling better." Isn't that just amazing? Bill really believed he was going to be healed here on this earth.

One of the things that Bill said over and over again during his cancer journey was "God's got this." He found a T-shirt that he liked and wore it frequently to chemotherapy. Thanks to the generosity of my brother Steve Fowler and his business, Imprinted Sportswear, I had T-shirts made up to give away to lots of family members and friends. No matter what you may be going through, I pray that you never forget Bill's words. "God's got this!" He knew it. He believed it. He found hope in those words, and you can too.

In closing, I would just like to ask each of you to make time today to draw close to the Lord. No one knows what the future holds. One of the reasons why Bill and I were able to get through those cancer years is because our faith in God was already nailed into place. We had already developed a daily discipline of reading from His Word. We had experienced firsthand the value of quiet time in prayer each day with the Lord. As we drew closer to the Lord, He drew closer to us. When cancer hit, we were already in a very good place spiritually. Don't wait until you receive bad news to get right with the Lord or draw closer to Him. Don't wait until the storm hits to nail down your faith in Christ.

I know that God has numbered each of our days. He and He alone knows how many more days we will have on this earth. I pray that Bill's life and the legacy he left will convict and motivate each of us to an even deeper level of walk with Christ.

> But thanks be to God! He gives us the victory through our Lord Jesus Christ. (1 Corinthians 15:57 NIV)

Two years. Two years since I last held your hand. Two years since I kissed your sweet face. Two years since I heard you whisper that you loved me. The time without you has been so difficult, Bill. I love you so much. I am so thankful for the promise of heaven—just knowing I will see you again and we will spend all of eternity together. #besthusbandever

9 781664 283862